THE MANY FACETS OF
LEADERSHIP

Martin McCormack

redOystor

London | Johannesburg | New York

First Published by Martin McCormack 2014
First Edition ISBN: 978-0-9226988-2-9
Second Publication by RedOystor Books 2018
    an Imprint of RedOystor Media (Pty) Ltd

Published by RedOystor Books
an imprint of RedOystor Media (Pty) Ltd

visit www.redoystor.com for more information
Or contact us at www.redoystor.com/contact-us

www.redoystor.com/Fecets-Of-Leadership

Commissioned by PrintHUB Swaziland (Pty) Ltd
Cover Design & Layout by RedOystor Media (Pty) Ltd

⊙ solutions
Printed by novus print, a Novus Holdings company

2nd Edition
ISBN: 978-0-9947217-4-7 (print)
      978-0-9947217-5-4 (Epub)

...Success in life involves self-development and utilising all your gifts...

About the Author

Martin McCormack is an Irish Salesian priest, living in Malkerns (Swaziland). He has been running leadership training for teachers and young people for 36 years. He has presented workshops in Ireland, Denmark, West Africa and Southern Africa.

He is a former High school teacher, inspirational speaker, life coach and Rotarian. He holds a Masters in Leadership, Pastoral care and management. He is the author of 'The many facets of leadership' and many other journals in history, folklore, grief and bereavement and pastoral care issues.

Martin runs a leadership academy in Malkerns and a women's empowerment programme at St Anne's High school Malkerns.

email: frmmccormack@gmail.com
cell: 00268-76993922 Swaziland

Table of Contents

LEADERSHIP

When you become a leader it is about
helping others to grow

Foreword

This book by Martin McComack is a 'must-read' for all people interested in an aspect of 'Leadership'. It contains a wealth of knowledge – both at an experiential and theoretical level.

The author uses a combination of his own experience as a leader on two continents: Europe and Africa. This book is about the many facets of leadership in different situations.

Martin McComack's own leadership from working in different areas of life, coupled with his theoretical knowledge provides the reader with a down-to-earth detailed account of the many facets of leadership.

The content in the book incorporates many focuses of leaders and leadership. Among the topic covered include tips on how to become a leader, leadership theories, the qualities needed for leadership, inspirational leadership, peer leadership, moral leadership and servant leadership.

The book is sprinkled throughout with humorous stories and allegories reflecting the author's personality.

'The many Facets of Leadership' can be used as a self-help book or as a comprehensive reference book or even as an aid for questions and answers in a Table Quiz!

It is suitable for anyone already in a leadership role or who is interested in pursuing one. Empowering others to become leaders is a worthwhile legacy for those who come after us. We are not born leaders but we can be!

Marjorie Fitzpatrick PhD

All Hallows College
Dublin – April 2014

Introduction

Success in life involves self-development and utilising all your gifts. When you become a leader it is about helping others to grow.

Harry S. Truman said: In periods where there is no leadership society stands still. Progress occurs when courageous, skilful leaders seize the opportunity to change things for the better.[1]

Over the past 30 years I have run leadership training courses in Ireland, South Africa, Swaziland, Lesotho and West African countries. When I started off I found it very difficult to get material I could use and adapt to the needs of the various groups. This book is the gleanings and the sweepings of my own learning.

I offer it as a resource for teachers, youth workers and anyone working in leadership development. It is something you

1. http://www.brainyquote.com/

can dip into for a good quote, a story, a poem or reflection and some general academic information on leadership issues.

I have very deliberately steered away from taking a purely academic approach to leadership. There are already excellent works published in the academic field.

In my own journey through life I have been influenced by St. John Bosco, the founder of the Salesian congregation. I will speak about him in the context of servant leaders.

I have met some wonderful leaders in my lifetime and been privileged to work alongside some of them. The chapters that follow offer some of my learning. I hope you enjoy the read and find moments of inspiration for your own leadership.

"Be The One"

> Be the one to be strong
> and turn heads around
> Even from dark to light
> You are the spark
> You have the fire
> You are the heart
> Now be a believer
> Don't get lost in the crowd

Author: Unknown

Acknowledgments:

Thank you to Jean O'Sullivan for corrections, proof reading and insightful comments.

Thank you to Dr. Marjorie Fitzpatrick for her continuous encouragement, support and insights.

Thank you to Lorraine Moroney, Fitzsomons Printers (for the first print), her advice and assistance.

Chapter One

What is Leadership?

All men dream, but not equally. Those who dream by night in the dusty recesses of their minds wake in the day to find that it was vanity: but the dreamers of the day are dangerous men, for they may act their dream with open eyes to make it possible. (E.Lawrence)1

In this first chapter we will examine leadership positions and characteristics, explore what leadership is and examine charismatic leadership.

We have all sorts of notions about who should lead and what qualities leaders should have. The 'perfect' leader with all the desirable qualities has not yet been born. The following story is a good illustration of criticism and negativity around leadership and shows just how difficult it is to be in a position of leading others.

1   T. E Lawrence, Seven Pillars of Wisdom, 1997, Anchor

The chairman of the Church Board received the following chain letter in the mail:

2 This chain letter is meant to bring you happiness.

Unlike other chain letters, it does not cost money.

Sit down and make a list of five other churches that are tired of their ministers. Send a copy of this letter to all five churches on the list.

Then send your minister to the church on the bottom of the list. In one week you will receive 15,625 ministers and one of them should be a hit! Have faith in this letter.

P.S. Please don't break the chain. In fact, one church broke the chain and they got their old minister back.

History gives us a rather interesting account on resolution of leadership conflict.

For example, the French novelist and playwright Alexander Dumas once had a heated quarrel with a rising young politician.

The argument became so intense that a duel was inevitable.

Since both men were superb shots they decided to draw lots, the loser agreeing to shoot himself. Dumas lost. Pistol in hand he withdrew in silent dignity to another room, closing the door behind him.

The rest of the company waited in gloomy suspense for the shot that would end his career. It rang out at last.

His friends ran to the door, opened it and found Dumas, smoking revolver in hand. "Gentlemen, a most regrettable thing has happened," he announced. "I missed."[3]

---

2   www.sermoncentral.com/.../humorous-illustrations-about-Church-Genera...
3   www.sermonillustrations.com/a-z/c/conflict

DIFFERENT LEADERSHIP POSITIONS

Leadership can be approached from different perspectives; one of which is reflected in the account below:

A man is flying in a hot air balloon and realises he is lost.

He reduces height and spots a man down below.

He lowers the balloon further and shouts, "Excuse me, can you tell me where I am?" The man below says "Yes, you're in a hot air balloon, hovering 30 feet above this field. You are between 40 & 42 degrees North latitude and between 58 & 60 degrees West longitude."

"You must work in information technology," says the balloonist. "I do," says the man, "but how did you know?" "Well," says the balloonist, "everything you have told me is technically correct but it's of no use to me."

The man below says "You must be a corporate manager." "I am," replies the balloonist, "but how did you know?" "Well," says the man, "you don't know where you are or where you're going but you expect me to be able to help.

You're in the same position you were before we met but now it's my fault."

What is leadership?

There are many different definitions of what 'leadership' is.[4]

> **Leadership** is about shaping beliefs, desires and priorities. It is about achieving influence, not securing compliance.[5]

> **Leadership** therefore needs to be distinguished from such things as management, decision making and authority. [6]

> **Leading** is to live dangerously because when you lead peo-

---

4   S. Alexander Haslam, Stephen D. Reicher, Michael J. Platow. The New Psychology of Leadership: Identity, Influence and Power 2001 p ix.
5   ibid p. x
6   ibid p. x

ple through difficult change, you challenge what people hold dear; their daily habits, tools, loyalties and ways of thinking, with nothing more to offer than a possibility. It is no wonder that when the myriad opportunities to exercise leadership call, we hesitate.[7]

> **Effective leadership** involves influencing others so they are motivated to achieve group goals. This is at the heart of any progress. [8]

There are many ideas also about the characteristics of 'leadership'[9]

> Leadership is something special. It is found in people who want to better themselves, their clubs, schools and society.

> Leadership is not selfish. It reaches out to others, sets a good example and shows others the best 'in them' and inspires them to seek the best 'in life' and in others.

> Leadership is generosity in action. It respects others, it is not overpowering and it is not an ego trip.

> We all need leadership in ourselves, so we can realise we have to use our talents, give of ourselves and be open to possibilities.

> We need leadership in others because we are not supermen or superwomen. We need to be directed. We need to see the greatness in others so we can be encouraged always to keep trying and to keep living fully our own potential.

'Leaders' have the following characteristics, some leaders have all, and some have a few:[10]

> **Leaders** take responsibility when the opportunity is at hand. They carry out a job without fanfare.

> **Leaders** are going places because they are always on the move.

> **Leaders** are alert to the situations that might call for help.

7   ibid p. x
8   ibid p. x
9   Author unknown
10 www.lionsclubs.org.au/201q1/Newsletters/55.Feb10.pdf,p 1.

> **Leaders** know how to talk. They realise that talking is an important way of communicating, especially if they talk with confidence, reason and patience.

> **Leaders** think before they speak. They speak with intelligence and sincere honesty.

> **Leaders** know there is a time and place for everything. There is a time to be serious, a time to joke, a time to relax, a time to work and a time to play.

> Above all **leaders** have the unique sensitivity to know exactly when the time is for these things.

> **Leaders** dare to be different. That is why leaders really live. Life is always something of a mysterious hush. It is something of a gift.

> **Leaders** want to be part of this thing called life.

Charles Handy[11] writes that 'Leadership' has affected political systems, education, institutions and organisations. He states that:

1. Approaches to the problem of leadership have usually 'fallen into one of three general headings: trait theories, style theories and contingency theories. Each has an element of truth but in the final analysis fail to explain the difference between effective and ineffective leaders.

2. Leadership is multidimensional- an amalgam of many different components.

3. Effective leadership requires a balanced mixture of good theory and skills. It involves influencing others so they are motivated to contribute to the achievement of the group goals.

4. New psychology sees leadership as "a product of an individual's *we-ness* rather than his or her *I-ness*" This forces us to see leadership not as a process revolving around

11 Charles Handy, 1999, p.36

individuals, acting and thinking in isolation, but as a group process in which leaders and followers are joined together and perceive themselves as joined together.

S. I. McMillen, in his book None of These Diseases,[12] tells a story of a young woman who wanted to go to college but her heart sank when she read the question on the application form that asked "Are you a leader?"

Being both honest and conscientious, she wrote "No" and returned the application, expecting the worst.

To her surprise, she received this letter from the college "Dear Applicant: A study of the application forms reveals that this year our college will have 1,452 new leaders. We are accepting you because we feel it is imperative that they have at least one follower."

Characteristics of charismatic leaders

The above story shows that everywhere we have leaders; we have those who are led. But is there such a leader as a 'Charismatic' leader?

A 'charismatic' leader captures popular imagination and inspires allegiance and devotion. Charismatic leaders are people who have a divinely inspired gift, grace and talent and a magnetic appeal.

Charismatic leaders are said to articulate a vision people will buy into. They present a vision of the future.13

They bring together the past and the future by letting followers fill in how they intend to act in the present in order to achieve that vision.

They spend time talking to followers.

12 S. I. McMillen (Author), David E., M.D. Stern (Editor), None of These Diseases June 1, 1984
13 *www.stitcher.com/podcast/brand-fasttrackers*

They replace their personal goals with those of the collective and exude confidence in other's ability to 'realise the bigger picture'.[14] Followers of charismatic leaders have a higher sense of collective identity in their self-concept.

They undertake actions on behalf of the leader and the collective; they believe in what they are doing and have a sense of meaningfulness.[15] Weber[16] defines charismatic leadership as 'resting on devotion to the exceptional sanctity, heroism or exemplary character of an individual person and of the normative patterns or order revealed or ordained by him.'

He envisaged religious leaders like Jesus as charismatic leaders. Later researchers considered various socio-political leaders such as Mahatma Ghandi, Martin Luther King Jr., Winston Churchill, John. F. Kennedy and Nelson Mandela as charismatic leaders. They were essentially very skilled communicators – individuals who were verbally eloquent but also able to communicate to followers on a deep, emotional level. They were able to articulate a compelling or captivating vision and were able to arouse strong emotions in followers.

Charismatic leadership is leadership based on the leader's capability to converse and behave in ways that reach followers in ways that motivate and inspire.

A charismatic leader should have the gift to speak on a very commanding emotional level.

Charismatic leaders appeal strongly to the values of the followers and it is the psychological bondage between the two which makes the leader succeed.

There is a great example of this in the movie 'Any Given Sunday' where Al Pacino delivers a charismatic speech appealing to the values of his team.

14 ibid
15 P.T. Joseph. 2010, p.171.
16 Weber, 1968, p. 245, 252

AL PACINO'S INCH BY INCH SPEECH [17]

I don't know what to say really.
Three minutes to the biggest battle of our professional
lives all comes down to today.
Either we heal as a team or we are going to crumble,
Inch by inch play by play till we're finished.
We are in hell right now, gentlemen
believe me we can stay here
and get the shit kicked out of us

OR

We can fight our way back into the light.
We can climb out of hell.
One inch, at a time.
Now I can't do it for you.
I'm too old.
I look around and I see these young faces
and I think, I mean

I made every wrong choice a middle age man could
make. I uh....I pissed away all my money
believe it or not.
I chased off anyone who has ever loved me.

And lately, I can't even stand the face I see in the mirror.
You know when you get old in life
things get taken from you.
That's, that's part of life.
But, you only learn that when you start losing stuff.
You find out that life is just a game of inches.
So is football. Because in either game life or football

The margin for error is so small.
I mean one half step too late or too early
you don't quite make it.
One half second too slow or too fast
and you don't quite catch it.
The inches we need are everywhere around us.

They are in every break of the game
every minute, every second.
On this team, we fight for that inch
On this team, we tear ourselves, and everyone around us
to pieces for that inch.
We CLAW with our finger nails for that inch.
Cause we know
when we add up all those inches
that's going to make the fucking difference
between WINNING and LOSING
between LIVING and DYING.
I'll tell you this
in any fight
it is the guy who is willing to die
who is going to win that inch.
And I know if I am going to have any life anymore
it is because, I am still willing to fight, and die for that
inch because that is what LIVING is.
The six inches in front of your face.

Now I can't make you do it.
You gotta look at the guy next to you.
Look into his eyes.
Now I think you are going to see a guy who will go that
inch with you.

You are going to see a guy
who will sacrifice himself for this team
because he knows when it comes down to it,
you are gonna do the same thing for him.

That's a team, gentlemen
and either we heal now, as a team,
or we will die as individuals.
That's football guys.
That's all it is.
Now, whataya gonna do?

Hungarian born American film and stage actress, Zsa Zsa Gabor) said that she never hated a man enough to give him back his diamonds and she received diamonds from 9 husbands.[18]

Diamonds are rare and they are hard to find. They come to the surface of the earth during volcanic eruptions in a bluish substance called kimberlite.

Charismatic leaders are like diamonds, rare and unique, each having their own facets of strength.

Charismatic leaders create an atmosphere of change and present an idealized vision of the future that is better than what exists currently. They communicate their ideas in such a way that everyone can identify and comprehend. They inspire followers with a faith to bring about change.

The source of power in a charismatic leader comes from personal power rather than positional power.

Although charismatic leaders may be in positions of authority, the leadership transcends this and is influenced by personal qualities rather than the power and authority given by the group.

Bernard Bass[19] lists the following characteristics for a 'charismatic' leader:

1. Expressive behaviour
2. Self-confidence
3. Self-determination
4. Insight
5. Freedom from internal conflict
6. Eloquence
7. High energy level

One such 'Charismatic' leader is John Bosco.

---

19 Bernard Bass, cited in Pt. Joseph., 2010, p.170

Chapter Two

John Bosco

There is an Old Chinese proverb which says:

A leader is someone you choose to follow to a place you wouldn't go by yourself. The role of the leader is to recognize the future. The role of the leader is to find the future. The role of the leader is to secure the future. If you want 1 year of prosperity, grow grain. If you want 10 years of prosperity, grow trees. If you want 100 years of prosperity, grow people.[1] The wisdom of the Chinese proverb for a prosperous future points the way for leadership development.

This chapter gives a short overview of St. John Bosco, founder of the Salesian Order. His vision of life has inspired thousands across the world. When he was a child he had a dream and this dream developed into a worldwide movement for young people. His particular style of leadership will be presented. Bosco believed that all young people were special and if given encouragement could have great influence on other young people.

Over the past thirty years I have been training young people in leadership skills and encouraging them to reach out across the world to other young people. I begin training workshops with this poem 'I'm special'.[2]

Coming in contact with the vision of Don Bosco led me down the road I have followed in life reaching out to young people where ever I have worked.

We are all special and good leaders help us discover our own uniqueness. In 1972 I picked up a GAA magazine and in the middle of it I saw a picture of St. John Bosco. I wrote to the college and got his story and was fascinated with his life.

I saw parallels with my own story. Several months later I went as a Leaving Cert student to Salesian College Ballinakill and then joined the followers of Bosco in the Salesian congregation. This choice has given me opportunities to lead in many parts of the world.

Who was John Bosco?

John Bosco was the youngest son of Francesco Bosco (1784–1817) and Margherita Occhiena. He had two older brothers, Antonio and Giuseppe (1813–1862).

The Boscos of Becchi were farmhands of the Biglione Family who lived close by. The full responsibility of the family passed to the widow Margherita when her husband Francis died.

This was in a time of great shortage and famine in the Piedmont countryside after the devastation of the Napoleonic wars and the long drought which lasted from 1817 to 1819. St. John Bosco is remembered as a man who dedicated his life to the service of abandoned young people.

He was driven by first hand experience of the effects of dreadful poverty and hunger of the young people he came across. Others were inspired to follow him in responding to the needs of the young.

John Bosco created an Order in the Catholic Church called the Salesians.[3]

Through a series of events in his youth, not least a very powerful dream he had as a young boy, he learned to become a leader for the young people he grew up with, many of whom were very badly behaved. In order to relate to them he needed to develop certain skills.

He learned that by combining entertainment with teaching and praying he could achieve positive results.

Entertained by his magical balancing act, the young people would gladly listen to a lesson or pray with John Bosco.[4] John Bosco had a dream which he relates as that which provided the inspiration for his vocation:

John Bosco's Dream[5]

It was at the age of nine that I had a dream. A crowd of children were playing there. Some were laughing, some were playing games and quite a few were swearing.

When I heard these evil words, I jumped immediately amongst them and tried to stop them by using my words and my fists. At that moment a dignified man appeared a nobly dressed adult. He wore a white cloak and his face shone so that

3   John A. Morrison 1979, p.3
4   Memories of the Oratory. 1966, Vol 1. P.29, ff.
5   Memoria Biography" 1815 pps. 3, 4

I could not look directly at him. He called me by name, told me to take charge of these children and added these words: "You will have to win these friends of yours not by blows but by gentleness and love.

Start right away to teach them the ugliness of sin and the value of virtue." Confused and frightened, I replied that I was a poor, ignorant child. I was unable to talk to those youngsters about religion. At that moment the kids stopped their fighting, shouting and swearing; they gathered round the man who was speaking.

Hardly knowing what I was saying, I asked, "Who are you, ordering me to do the impossible?" "Precisely because it seems impossible to you, you must make it possible through obedience and the acquisition of knowledge." "Where, by what means, can I acquire knowledge?"

"I will give you a teacher. Under her guidance you can become wise. Without her, all wisdom is foolishness."

"But who are you that speak so?" "I am the son of the woman whom your mother has taught you to greet three times a day."

The dream becomes an inspiration

This dream continued to be a guiding force throughout his life. It affected his whole way of thinking and acting and experiencing the presence of God.[6]

It inspired him to become a priest. In 1841, just short of his 26th birthday, he was ordained. In Italy, priests are called 'Don'[7] followed by their family name, so John Bosco became Don Bosco.

---

6   Pietro Stella 1985, p.10
7   Lemoyne, Vol. 11, Memories of Oratory, p. 311

The Dream develops

Upon becoming a priest, Don Bosco realised how he needed to live out his vocation. The Industrial Revolution was spreading into Northern Italy; there was a great deal of poverty, desolation, turmoil and people lived in hopelessness.

Bosco became completely focussed on his vocation when he entered the prisons. He wrote: 'To see so many children, from 12 to 18 years of age, all healthy, strong, intelligent, lacking spiritual and material food was something that horrified me.'[8]

Bosco realised how his dream and the guidance it gave were needed. He knew a new approach was required. Frederick Buecherner asserts that vocation is 'The place where your deep gladness meets the world's need.'[9] In the ensuing years Bosco would show this.

The dream becomes a system

Don Bosco knew that education was the key to helping these young people. He sought to teach them and to get fairer treatment for them with their employers. He looked to help other young people who still slept under bridges and on the streets.

Even when they stole from him, as some did, he never gave up hope. He never lost his confidence in youth. Don Bosco started technical schools to educate the young people in skilled jobs like printing, bookbinding and mechanics.

In those days, these were the skills that would guarantee better conditions and a better future for them.

He published numerous works which included '*The key to heaven for practicing Catholics*', '*The Companion of youth*' and '*The Fundamentals of Catholic religion*'.

8   J. A. Lenti, 2007, Vol. 2, p.14ff
9   Parker .J Palmer, 2000, p.16

The Preventive system

The heart of the Salesian tradition of education is called "Preventive System".[10] This was the name given to Don Bosco's style of education after a lecture that he gave to his French co-operators in 1887 in which he contrasted the Preventive system with what he characterised as the "Repressive System".[11]

Empowerment is a modern term used in educational discussion to focus on enabling the learner to become independent and self-motivated.

In that lecture Bosco took the view that fear as a motivating force for children was disabling and hence a system based on punishments failed to win over or change the hearts of the young or help them to learn.

Therefore, he counselled the educator to try to win over the hearts of the young by becoming an animating presence among them.[12] His system was based on "Reason-Religion-Relationship" with the young.[13]

One should always begin with what the young enjoyed, especially in terms of games and active recreations as well as music, singing and theatre and bring them gradually to a deeper awareness of the beautiful, the true and the good and thus to God, the Giver of all that is Good.

The context in which Don Bosco first evolved his system was that of the Oratory which was of its nature both a voluntary and energy flowing youth activity.[14] Assistance in that context meant getting the youngsters involved in the various activities and noticing when they were losing interest and moving them on to something else, gradually seeing the opportunity for a

10 J.A. Lenti 2008, Vol. 3 pps.143, 156
11 John A. Morrison 1979, p. 90
12 ibid pps.111-116
13 ibid, p.92
14 ibid pps. 92, 93

word in the ear and the catechism and worship which was at the heart of the activities.[15]

The stories of the clerics, Rua and Cagliero, shocking the Turinese clergy by running through the streets on the way to their various assignments in the city's oratories speak of a freshness of approach and an energy and vigour that characterised the emergence of the preventive style of education.

Sensitive leadership was the principle that guided the young Salesians and quickly involved them in looking after and leading others.

Bosco's Peer Leadership

Bosco's famous sodalities were training sessions for peer mentors or youth leaders who were engaged in the same apostolic enterprise with Don Bosco. In Don Bosco's practice this presence-assistance among the young was a creative and active way of engaging young people at the Oratory in a friendly relationship and building future leaders for society.[16]

What began as a technique for outreach to young people from the streets that had lost their trust and confidence in adults became a form of almost complete supervision and control.

'Letting the youngsters know the rules of the Institute and then assisting them without respite, by advising them, by guiding them, and correcting them' or in other words as he concluded 'in putting them in the impossibility of committing faults 'mancanze', which could also be translated as sins.'[17]

The preventive system was based on four pillars: devotion to Mary Help of Christians, devotion to Jesus in the Eucharist, an

15 ibid p.93
16 ibid, pps. 69-70, 107-8, 120, 123, 169-71
17 Quoted in F. Desramaut Spiritualita Salesiana: Cento Parole Chiave LAS, Roma, 2001, p.573.

educational system based on joy, hope and devotion to Church and Vicar of Christ. With these four spiritual indicators, Salesian education offers to society and to the Church good Christians as well as honest citizens.[18]

The burden of care grew. Bosco gathered around him men and women, willing to share their lives with the young and the poor.

He chose Francis de Sales as patron for his gentleness and patience to guide them and Michael Rua as the first Salesian leader. As well as being a charismatic leader John Bosco could also be considered a 'servant leader'.

But what is a 'servant leader'?

18 Pietro, Stella.1985, p.180 ff. & J. A. Lenti 2009, Vol. 6 pp.51 ff

Chapter Three

Servant Leadership

A 2000 Year Old Chinese Poem says: Go to the people, Learn from them. Love them. Start with what they know. Build on what they have. But of the best leaders, when their task is accomplished and their work is done, the people will remark:"We have done it ourselves".'[1]

Modern society speaks a lot about the need for service to humanity. Cynics say leaders are only feathering their own nests and leaders don't care about the people.

There is a certain truth in this from my experience in various countries. Servant leadership however offers a challenge to this cynicism.

This chapter explores the history and significance of this type of leadership. It explores the notion of oppression and examines the characteristics of being a servant leader.

1   http://en.wikipedia.org/wiki/Servant_leadership

At the end it presents some truths worth following and offers beatitudes of leadership.

I was on the train one afternoon and there was a gentleman talking very loudly on his mobile. To all of us listening he seemed to be doing a business deal. In the middle of his conversation his phone rang and we laughed at the notion of his imaginary conversation making him look an idiot. To be an effective leader one has to be honest with oneself and stop trying to convince others that we are something we are not. The following story is a good illustration.[2]

The young lawyer's mind was racing as he pictured himself working cases and arguing before juries. He was extremely excited. As he went into his new office he went over to his oversized oak desk and sat in his desk chair that was an executive leather chair fit for only the very best, highly successful lawyers. He leaned back and began to day dream some more.

Just as he was deep in thought he heard and then saw a person come in the front door by the empty reception area. Quickly leaning forward he grabbed the telephone and began pretending he was speaking with someone on the other end of the telephone about a complex law case. Knowing that the man in the reception area could hear him he spoke louder than normal trying to appear as important as possible.

He was able to keep up this act for about two to three minutes before he winded down the fake conversation and finally hanging up the telephone. After hanging up he walked out to the reception area and apologized for keeping the man waiting. Still trying to impress the potentially new client he went on to tell the man that it was very hard to keep up with all the telephone calls while he was searching for another prominent attorney to bring on board with him.

2   Robert K. Greenleaf, Servant Leadership: A Journey into the Nature of Legitimate Power and Greatness. Indianapolis: The Robert K. Greenleaf Center, 1970

The brand new lawyer told the man that just any other attorney would not be good enough, he only wanted the best. After going on about just how important the call was the he had just been on he asked the man how he could help him. The man smiled a bit and told the young lawyer that he was only there to hook up his telephones.

The contrast of the two people in this story is striking. The first is presenting a public persona that is false. The second is there to provide a service and waits patiently while the charade is going on. Servant leadership invites us to focus on the needs of the other person.

History of Servant Leadership

The general concept is ancient. Chanakya[3] wrote in the 4th century B.C. in his book Arthashastra "the king [leader] shall consider as good, not what pleases himself but what pleases his subjects [followers]" "the king [leader] is a paid servant and enjoys the resources of the state together with the people."

There are passages that relate to servant leadership in the Tao Te Ching, attributed to Lao-Tzu, who is believed to have lived in China sometime between 570 B.C. and 490 B.C.[4]:

The highest type of ruler is one of whose existence the people are barely aware. Next comes one whom they love and praise. Next comes one whom they fear. Next comes one whom they despise and defy.

When you are lacking in faith, others will be unfaithful to you. The Sage is self-effacing and scanty of words. When his task is accomplished and things have been completed, all the people say, 'we ourselves have achieved it'.[5]

3 http://en.wikipedia.org/wiki/Arthashastra
4 https://leadershiparlington.org/pdf/TheServantasLeader.pd by RK Greenleaf
5 www.forbes.com/sites/.../why-isn't-servant-leadership-more-prevalent

Williams[6] in 2002 in discussing 'servant leadership' notes that servant leaders tend to avoid the limelight and work behind the scenes.

Leadership may simply consist of listening to someone who is having a difficulty or making a quiet suggestion to someone or drawing attention to their problem. The phrase "servant leadership" was coined by Robert K. Greenleaf.[7]

> It requires an understanding of identity, mission, vision and environment. A servant leader is someone who is servant first, who has responsibility to be in the world, and so he contributes to the well-being of people and community. A servant leader looks to the needs of the people and asks himself how he can help them to solve problems and promote personal development. He places his main focus on people, because only content and motivated people are able to reach their targets and to fulfil the set expectations.

In *The Servant as Leader*, an essay that he first published in 1970,[8] Greenleaf writes:

> The servant-leader is servant first. It begins with the natural feeling that one wants to serve. Then conscious choice brings one to aspire to lead. That person is sharply different from one who is leader first; perhaps because of the need to assuage an unusual power drive or to acquire material possessions. The leader-first and the servant-first are two extreme types.
>
> Between them there are shadings and blends that are part of the infinite variety of human nature. The difference manifests itself in the care taken by the servant-first

6   The Servant-Leader Within: A Transformative Path. Com/the-servant-leader-within-transformative-path-by-499.
7   Pdf. Servant leadership: the leadership theory of Robert K. Greenleaf, http://www.carolsmith.us/downloads/640greenleaf.pdf
8   Servant as Leader essay, Robert K. Greenleaf

to make sure that other people's highest priority needs are being served.

The best test, and difficult to administer, is: Do those served grow as persons? Do they, while being served, become healthier, wiser, freer, more autonomous, more likely themselves to become servants? And what is the effect on the least privileged in society? Will they benefit or at least not be further deprived?

The idea for his essay, "The Servant as Leader," came out of reading Hesse's Journey to the East.[9] The story is about a travel group on an exceptional mythical journey. The main character of this story is Leo. Leo is the companion and servant of the group but he also sustains them with his charisma and spirit and gives them well-being.

Everything was going well until Leo disappears; the group fall apart and the journey has to be prematurely interrupted. The group cannot exist longer without their servant Leo.

Servant leadership seeks to involve others in decision making, is strongly rooted in ethical and caring behaviour and enhances the personal growth of workers while improving the care and quality of community life.

There are several characteristics of the servant- leader:[10]

> Servant leadership has potential for healing oneself and others
> Self-awareness strengthens the servant-leader
> It relies on persuasion rather than on positional authority
> He listens deeply to others
> He strives to understand and empathise with others
> Servant leaders dream great dreams and can look beyond day to day realities

9 The Journey to the East - Hermann Hesse.pdf - Ning
10 LC Spears (1998) 'Tracing the growing impact of servant-leadership'. In: L Spears (ed.) Insights on Leadership. John, Wiley. 50

Foresight is a characteristic that enables the servant leader to understand the lessons from the past, the realities of the present and the likely consequences of a decision for the future.

In his second major essay, *The Institution as Servant*, Robert K. Greenleaf[11] articulated what is often called the "credo." He said:

> This is my thesis: caring for persons, the more able and the less able serving each other, is the rock upon which a good society is built.

> Whereas, until recently, caring was largely person to person, now most of it is mediated through institutions - often large, complex, powerful and, impersonal; not always competent; sometimes corrupt.

> If a better society is to be built, one that is more just and more loving, one that provides greater creative opportunity for its people, then the most open course is to raise both the capacity to serve and the very performance as servant of existing major institutions by new regenerative forces operating within them.

Leadership style

In the 6th Century BC Lao Tzu[12] stated that 'The leader is a teacher who succeeds without taking credit. And, because credit is not taken, credit is received'.

John Bosco's life was centred on "Servant Spirituality". This was seen in his educative methodology. He followed a mystical path of prophetic vocation, friendship with God, a life-long concern for the young. "Servant spirituality" was his prophetic call.

11 https://greenleaf.org/what-is-servant-leadership/-the-Greenleaf-centre-
12 http://www.susangerke.com/quotes.html

Bosco was grounded in loving kindness, gentleness, compassion, care and concern, and his commitments were shaped by these very human qualities. It was a spirituality of the heart that served human and spiritual wholeness. His style of leadership served life and justice and stood in contrast to repressive, dominator models in life.

Leadership meant seeking the spirit in order to engage the human spirit in the search for meaning, integrity, identity and the core self.[13] "Servant spirituality" taught him to put young people who were in poverty first. It led him to be a teacher, a bearer of inspiration, a model of faith in touch with the deep questions of the human spirit.

He was servant, a guide, one who offered invitations and proposals, not a disciplinarian. He offered a vision grounded and made real in personal dedication.

The young knew they were in the presence of someone who was on their side, whose values, experiences and assumptions could be taken to heart.

He entered through the heart and encouraged the mind. However, Bosco was a realist. He knew that he could not draw all the young people he met to be honest citizens and good Christians but he did not stop trying.

He never lost hope of winning hearts for God. Bosco is a man of many colours: priest, saint, founder, mystic and prophet, servant of the young and the poor, educator, pastor, social activist, evangelist, healer, writer.

"He is a man aflame with the glowing fire of Sinai shining through myriad activities, talents and charismatic gifts; truly a man of God wrapped in an ecstasy of love-filled and hope-filled action with a world-wide reach."[14]

13 Jack Finnegan, October 2012 Don Bosco Educator: p.6, paraphrased.
14 ibid p.8.

Characteristics of servant leadership

Stephen Covey[15] writes that when team members regard each other with mutual respect, differences are utilized and are considered strengths rather than weaknesses.

The role of the leader is to foster mutual respect and build a complementary team where, each strength is made productive and each weakness irrelevant.

The Greeks used to describe leadership as 'diakonia' which means 'to wait at table'.[16] A gospel example is Jesus washing the feet of the disciples. This is summed up in Matthew's Gospel[17] 'I have given you an example that you may copy what I have done to you'.

Servant leadership is modelled after the attributes of Jesus Christ and energized to action by the Holy Spirit. Jesus Christ was the ultimate example of a leader who took on the form of a servant and humbled himself, even to death on the cross, in order to fulfil his Father's redemptive plan for humanity.

Certain characteristics are central to servant leadership.

They know God values us. Jesus was able to wash the grime from his disciple's feet. They find joy in encouraging and supporting team members. This enables others to develop their gifts in the context of their work. They don't need credit for their ideas and visions.

Servant leaders are high on relationship and low on control and coercion. They shun the trappings of authority and status.

They base their authority on character rather than the position they occupy. Leadership in the Christian community is centred on empowerment of others to participate in the work of the community. Jesus shared his ministry with a small band

15 Stephen Covey, (1990) *Principled Centred Leadership*
16 http://www.gty.org/resources/positions/p12/answering-the-key-questions-about-deacons
17 Matthew 26:14-39 New Revised Standard Version

of disciples. He called them forth by name and instructed them in what they were to do. Their task was to 'go to the lost sheep of the house of Israel. Go and preach the kingdom of heaven is near'. (Matthew 10: 1-16)

The leadership of Jesus served others by supporting them to take leadership themselves.

In this century many authors have written about the characteristics of 'servant leadership'.

One such author is L. Spear.

Ten characteristics of servant Leadership

L. Spear, 2002, in 'Tracing the past, present and future of servant leadership' presents ten characteristics of the servant leader:[18]

1. **Listening:** There is a deep commitment to listening intently to others. The servant- leader seeks to identify the will of a group and to help clarify that will. He or she seeks to listen receptively to what is being said (and not said).

2. **Empathy:** The servant-leader strives to understand and empathize with others. The most successful servant-leaders are those who become skilled empathetic listeners.

3. **Healing:** One of the great strengths of servant- leadership is its potential for healing oneself and others. Many people have suffered emotional hurts and servant leadership recognizes this as an opportunity to 'make whole' those with whom they come in contact.

18 Character and Servant Leadership: Ten Characteristics of Effective...www.regent.edu/acad/global/publications/jvl/vol1.../Spears_ and at www.boundless.com › ... › Leadership › Other Leadership Perspectives

4. **Awareness:** General awareness, especially self- aware-ness, strengthens the servant-leader. Making commit-ment to foster awareness can be scary –you never know what you may discover.

5. **Persuasion:** Reliance on persuasion, rather than on one's positional authority, in making decisions within an organization. The servant-leader seeks to convince others rather than coerce compliance.

6. **Conceptualization:** Servant–leaders seek to nurture their abilities to 'dream great dreams'. The ability to look at the problem from a conceptualizing perspective means that one must think beyond day-to-day realities.

7. **Foresight:** Foresight is a characteristic that enables the servant-leader to understand the lessons from the past, the realities of the present and the likely consequence of a decision for the future.

8. **Stewardship:** Holding something in trust for another. Servant-leadership, like stewardship, assumes first and foremost a commitment to serving the needs of others. It also emphasizes the use of openness and persuasion rather than control.

9. **Commitment to the growth of others:** Servant- leaders are deeply committed to the growth of each and every individual within his or her institution.

10. **Building community:** The servant- leader seeks to identify some means of building community among those who work within a given institution. Other au-thors write about leadership as a vocation.

Leadership as vocation

The idea of vocation lies at the heart of Christian spirituality. A vocation is first and foremost a relationship. Each person is called to engage with the mysteries of life and to see the otherness that lies at the heart of every individual. As a leader it is important to recognize one's own sense of vocation as an inner drive to make a difference in the lives of people.

The style we adopt, the concerns that energize us and the parts of leadership that expose our weakness will depend on our personal life story and the demands others make upon us.

A Christian leader will be prophetic, seeing the reality of the values around him or her and observing where the compromise happens.

Prophets are restless leaders because nothing is ever perfect. They will challenge compromises and be watchful figures in any team. Our present Pope Francis's style can be considered a 'Servant Leader'.

Pope Francis:

On March 19th, The Catholic Church inaugurated Cardinal Jorge Mario Bergoglio of Argentina as the 266th Pope. Since his election Pope Francis signalled, through his actions, a new direction for the Catholic church and a new style of leadership from the top.

Other leaders wishing to learn lessons in how to rebuild trust should watch carefully the approach of the new pontiff who has demonstrated humility, accessibility, vulnerability and a strong desire to articulate and share his vision at every opportunity. On Holy Thursday the Pope washed and kissed the feet of 12 prisoners at Casal Del Marmo on the outskirts of Rome.

He told those assembled there that everyone, including him, had to be in the service of others.

This concept of the servant leader is a strong signal about a person's view of leadership. It is not a position of power but rather that the leader demonstrates qualities that the people he leads want to follow and he, in turn, is dedicated to serving them.

He is showing a vulnerability that is challenging and refreshing. By choosing the name Francis after St. Francis of Assisi, the Pope revealed his intention to promote simplicity, the protection of the poor, humility and most importantly, the rebuilding of the Church. Pope Francis is exhibiting leadership through his humility and simplicity. In the teaching of Jesus the Beatitudes were presented as a map for living.

Although the author is unknown, the following presents a map for leadership, which Pope Francis endorses.

Beatitudes of a Leader[19]

1. Blessed is the leader who has not sought the high places but who has been drafted into service because of ability and willingness to serve.

2. Blessed is the leader who knows where they are going, why they are going and how they are going to get there.

3. Blessed is the leader who knows no discouragement, who presents no alibi.

4. Blessed is the leader who seeks the best for those he serves.

5. Blessed is the leader who leads for the good of the majority and not for personal gratification of his personal ideas.

19 Author unknown

6. Blessed is the leader who develops leaders while leading.

7. Blessed is the leader who marches with the group and correctly interprets the signs on the pathway that lead to success.

8. Blessed is the leader who has their head in the clouds and their feet on the ground.

9. Blessed is the leader who considers leadership an opportunity to serve.

There are various circumstances where leadership plays a vital role. One such circumstance is where people feel oppressed.

Leadership and oppression

Oppression is defined in several ways. Mullally[20] writes "oppression exists where people do not get equal treatment, or do not get treated with respect because they belong to certain group or category of people."

Oppression is a social phenomenon. He writes:

> What determines oppression is when a person is blocked from opportunities to self-development, is excluded from full participation in society, does not have certain rights that the dominant group takes for granted, or is assigned a second class citizenship, not because of individual talent, merit, or failure, but because of his or her membership in a particular group or category of people.

Sean Ruth[21] believes that a good leader thinks about the group's oppression, is aware of his or her own oppression and asks the question what are we like underneath the oppression.

There is internalised oppression in all of us.

20 Mullally2002, p.28 cited in Ruth, Leadership and Liberation p.116.
21 Sean Ruth. 2006 p.121

Leaders coming from outside a situation have not internalised that particular group oppression. They can see the pattern is not natural and find the origins of it.

A leader listens and thinks about the group. Rigidity comes from internalised hurts. The leader has to try to hear and see this hurt. People are inherently okay so by examining where they get messed up and why they are behaving in a particular way, the leader can model a new way and start a process of liberation.

"Liberation, as we see, does not mean simply changing the oppressed but also changing the ally and the oppressor."[22]

As leaders, we need to become aware of the ways negative feelings interfere with our ability to think clearly about people who are different to us.

As leaders we may have a lot of work to do to free ourselves from unconscious oppressive feelings, thoughts and behaviour. Doing this work is part of our leadership development.[23]

Ruth suggests that a servant leader has many characteristics. There are many types of leadership theories and models.

Today, the leader as well as being a "servant- leader" could be, as he suggests, a listener, a team builder, an enabler, a developer of other people and fundamentally a thinker.

There are certain truths about leadership.[24]

1. You have to believe that you can make a difference.

2. People have to believe in you if they are to follow you. You must have credibility.

3. People want to know what you stand for and believe in.

---

22 ibid p. 122
23 ibid pps. 122, 123
24 Santa Clara Magazine http://www.scu.edu/scm/article.cfm?b=439&c=12242

4. You have to take a long term perspective-focusing on the future sets effective leaders apart.

5. You can't do it alone-leadership is about collaboration.

6. Trust is what holds people together with a leader.

7. Effective leaders are always associated with changing the status quo.

8. You either lead by example or you don't lead at all.

9. The best leaders are the best learners.

10. Leaders love those whom they lead, the mission they serve and the world they do.

11. Truths in themselves are fine but without action nothing changes. Joseph Rost[25] presents a possible answer.

Leadership-from issue to action

Joseph Rost, in *Leadership for the Twenty First Century*, offers five insights into leadership. This type of leadership might prove invaluable in business or organizational change:

1. **Building the agenda**: Leaders and followers decide to take on a significant issue after debating the pros and cons of attempting to do something about the issue.

2. **Assessing the issue**: Leaders and followers gather and analyze information and reach conclusions about the direction they intend to take concerning the issue.

3. **Planning the change**: Leadership and followers develop an outline of the proposed change. The change reflects the mutual purposes of the leaders and followers.

4. **Gaining support**: Leaders and followers influence others in the organization to support the change. People in

25 Leadership for the twenty first century Joseph Roost_first_Century.html? Id=- bM7E8ORH-7QC&redir_esc=y

the organization influence each other on the specifics of the proposed change.

5. **Making the change**: Organizational policy makers decide on the proposed change. If the decision is positive, the staff members develop the strategies to institute the change in the organisation. If the decision is negative, the leaders and followers go back to square one. In order to have good leadership- it is necessary to become a good leader. But what is a good leader? In the next chapter we seek to find the answers.

Chapter Four

What makes a leader?

The very essence of leadership is [that] you have a vision. It's got to be a vision you articulate clearly and forcefully on every occasion. You can't blow an uncertain trumpet — Theodore Hesburgh[1]

Talk is cheap! There comes a time in life when each one of us is asked to take action. This involves taking up personal leadership and taking responsibility for getting things done.

There are too many people sitting on the fence of life expecting others to do what they are well capable of doing themselves.

In this chapter I want to look at a number of leadership issues. These include personal responsibility, the standardization of leadership, transactional and transformational leadership, liberation, fear and authority.

1   www.businessofwinning.com/resources_quotes.php?id=2

Let me begin with a poem to illustrate personal responsibility.

THAT'S NOT MY JOB[2]

This is a story told about four people named Somebody, Everybody, Anybody and Nobody.

There was one important job to be done.

Everybody was sure that somebody would do it but nobody did it. Somebody got angry about it because it was Everybody's job. Everybody thought anybody could do it.

Nobody realized that everybody wouldn't do it. It ended up that everybody blamed somebody when nobody did what anybody could have done. - **Author Unknown**

How do we get people to take responsibility and get involved in developing our society? How do we encourage more team and group participation in life?

It is interesting that there is no 'I' in the word team but much of our society is 'I' centered.

The movement from 'I' to 'we'[3] forces us to see leadership as a group process in which leaders and followers are joined together in shared endeavour. This has moved away from an earlier notion of the 'great man' approach. Alexander[4] suggests that:

> The broad view of leadership is its capacity to convince others to contribute to the processes that turn ideas and visions into reality and that help to bring about change. Leadership is always predicated on followership and the psychology of these two processes is inextricably intertwined.

2 www.budbilanich.com/the-story-of-everybody-somebody-anybody
3 Haslam et al, New Psychology of Leadership, 2011, p 2
4 ibid p.2

The Standardisation of Leadership

The research carried out on leadership personality types by Ralph Stogdill[5] showed them to be poor predictors of leadership and data emerged that the context of leadership dictates what qualities are required. Different contexts call for different forms of the same quality.

Stogdill observed that "the leader is likely to be more intelligent but not too much more intelligent than the group he led." This led him to state that the social situation was an important factor for leadership.

> A person does not become a leader by virtue of possession of some combination of traits, but the pattern of personal characteristics must bear some relevant relationship to the characteristics, activities and goals of the followers. Thus leadership must be conceived in terms of the interaction of variables which are in constant change and flux.

There is a diversity of opinion as to what makes a future leader. Wilkes suggests that one of Jesus' secrets was that he humbled 'his own heart'; while Murdock says he 'knew his own worth and went where he was celebrated.'[6]

Recent years have seen scholars rethinking their interest in the transformational quality of leadership. This theory holds that:

> At a particular time, a group of people have certain needs and requires the service of an individual to assist in meeting its needs. Which individual comes to play the role of leader in meeting these needs is essentially determined by chance, that is a given person happens to be at the critical place at the critical time.

5   R. M. Stogdill, Handbook of Leadership Theory, 1948, p.44.
6   Cooper & McGaugh, 1963, p.247, cited in Haslam, Alexander et al, p. 23

The particular needs of the group may, of course be best met when given time by an individual who possesses particular qualities. This does not mean that the particular individual's peculiar qualities would thrust him in a position of leadership in any other situation.

It means only that the unique needs of the group are met by the unique needs of the individual.[7]

This approach invites researchers to interpret events in terms of the broad social and structural conditions that prevail at a particular point in time.

This creates a situation where we cannot predict the form that leadership will need to take nor the form that follower will expect it to take because it depends on the unfolding reality.

Why is it that some leaders have big following and others get ignored? What is lacking is generally a vision that will transform people into followers and future leaders. Transactional leadership offers some insights.

Transactional and transforming leadership

Transformational leadership starts with the development of a vision, a view of the future that will excite and convert potential followers. The next step, which in fact never stops, is to constantly sell the vision.

This takes energy and commitment as few people will immediately buy into a radical vision and some will join the show much more slowly than others.

James McGregor Burns[8] suggests that the relations of most leaders and followers are termed "transactional-leaders" with followers exchanging one thing for another.

7   Haslam, Alexander et al, New Psychology of Leadership p. 12
8   J. M. Burns. Leadership, 1978.

The transforming leader recognises and exploits an existing need of a potential follower but beyond that the transforming leader looks for potential motives in followers, seeks to satisfy higher needs and engages the full person of the follower.

Further, the result of transforming leadership is a relationship of mutual stimulation and evaluation that converts followers into leaders and may convert leaders into moral agents.

Transactional leadership occurs when one person takes an initiative in making contact with others for the purpose of an exchange of valued things.

This exchange can be economic, political or psychological in nature. Each person recognises the other but that is as far as the relationship goes.

Transactional leaders:

> Build on the need to get a job done

> Are orientated to short-term goals and data

> Focus on tactical issues

> Rely on human relations to get the job done

> Support structures and systems that reinforce the bottom line

Primarily transactional leaders focus on performance outcomes. To that extent transactional leaders guide the contributors in the direction of establishing the established goal.

They will control ideas, help people interpret vision, values and strategy in a way that leads to success of the initiative.

Four words sum this style up: Control-Measurement- Administration-Performance. At times transactional leadership slips into bureaucratic leadership, where centralised authority, narrow spans of control and decision making follow a chain of command.

Contrasting this with transformational leadership, we see that such leadership occurs when one or more persons engage with others in such a way that leaders and followers raise one another to higher levels of motivation and morality. Their purposes become one. Transformational leadership becomes moral in that it raises the level of human conduct and ethical aspiration of both leader and led, thus it has a transforming effect on both.

James McGregor Burns writing on transformational leadership says true leadership arises from working with followers and is about much more than simply satisfying their wants and needs in exchange for support:

> Leaders hold enhanced influence at the higher levels of the need and value hierarchies. They can appeal to the more widely and deeply held value, such as justice, liberty and brotherhood.
>
> They can expose followers to the broader values that contradict narrower ones or inconsistent behaviour. They can redefine aspirations and gratifications to help followers see their stake in new program- orientated social movements[9]

Burns suggest that great leaders are people who are going on this developmental journey themselves but on the other hand their leadership is effective because it helps followers to go on the same journey. As the expression of needs become more purposeful leaders help transform followers' needs into positive hopes and aspirations.

One of the traps of Transformational Leadership is that passion and confidence can easily be mistaken for truth and reality.

Whilst it is true that great things have been achieved through enthusiastic leadership, it is also true that many passionate peo-

9 ibid p.43

ple have led the charge right over the cliff and into a bottomless chasm. Just because someone believes they are right, it does not mean they are right.[10]

In my training programmes I use a lot of games, situations and puzzles to get trainees thinking and working together. One such puzzle is called the memory quiz. Its primary function is to make people stop and think about how they perceive things.

Memory Quiz[11]

1. How do you put a giraffe into a refrigerator?

The correct answer is: Open the refrigerator, put in the giraffe and close the door.

This question tests whether you tend to do simple things in an overly complicated way.

2. How do you put an elephant into a refrigerator?

Wrong Answer: Open the refrigerator, put in the elephant and close the door.

Correct Answer: Open the refrigerator, take out the giraffe, put in the elephant and close the door.

This tests your ability to think through the repercussions of your actions.

3. The Lion King is hosting an animal conference; all the animals attend except one. Which animal does not attend?

Correct Answer: The Elephant. The Elephant is in the refrigerator. *This tests your memory.* Okay, even if you did not answer the first three questions correctly, you still have one more chance to show your abilities.

10 ibid p.117
11 www.superkids.com/aweb/pages/humor/12030.

4. **There is a river you must cross. But it is inhabited by crocodiles. How do you manage it?**

Correct Answer: You swim across. All the Crocodiles are attending the Animal Meeting!

This tests whether you learn quickly from your mistakes.

Leadership and Liberation

Another facet of leadership is that of leadership and liberation. Sean Ruth in his book Leadership and Liberation[12] proposes a different concept of leadership. He says people have to be thought about individually and collectively, about what is going on and what needs to happen.

Leadership draws people in collaboration.

A good leader has a picture of the possibilities for change and development in the people around them. In this sense vision is directly related to our ability to listen deeply and empathise.

Ruth continues about the importance of listening, indicating that listening builds relationships and then leadership becomes collaborative.

It is what we do, not our position. One can be in a leadership position and not leading.

We can lead without a title or authority. Leadership as a liberating process has many implications.

It is said that the most important job for any leader is to spot and train their own replacement and to make themselves redundant in that function as quickly as possible. [13] The test of any leadership training is how many leaders we leave behind after us.

12 Sean Ruth, Leadership and Liberation 2006
13 ibid p.28

I am very conscious of this question when I run workshops. What exactly am I modelling for the participants?

Over the years I have given serious consideration to these questions.

Working in an African culture has made me very aware that things are not always what they seem. Wisdom and age are highly respected in Africa.

When I was younger what I said was not taken too seriously because I was looked on as lacking experience.

Today, as the 'Umkhulu' grandfather, I carry huge leadership sway. I have learnt that one must seek first to understand the culture one is in, whether it's African or Irish, and be aware of how one is impacting on it. Sometimes things are not what they seem at first. This is summed up in the next section Model the Message.

Model the message[14]

One day a little old and very cute couple walked into the local fast food restaurant. The little old man went up to the counter and ordered their food. He brought back to the table a hamburger, a small amount of fries and a drink. Carefully he sliced the hamburger in two and then neatly divided the fries into two small piles.

He sipped the drink and then passed it to his wife. She took a sip and passed it back. A younger man at a nearby table observed this couple and began to feel sorry for them. He offered to buy them another meal but the old man respectfully declined saying that they were used to sharing everything.

The old man began to eat his food while his wife sat still not eating.

14 www.teamworkandleadership.com/.../seek-to-understand-first-fu

The young man continued to watch the old couple feeling there was something he should be doing to help. As the old man finished his half of the burger and fries, the old lady still had not started eating hers.

The young man couldn't take it anymore. He asked, "Ma'am, why aren't you eating?" The old lady looked up and politely said, pointing to the old man, "I'm waiting on the teeth." How many times are things not as they appear? Seek to understand first is a good rule of thumb.

What has been your experience as a leader with jumping to conclusions?

One of the characteristics of good leaders is that they model the message they preach. It's important that they demonstrate integrity in how they behave. Effective leaders model a sense of hope and encouragement for people.

They also model a belief and confidence in people around them. Nelson Mandela epitomized this. This modelling is not just pious platitudes. The type of relationship and behaviour of the leader are consistent with the values expressed by the leader.

Central to this is the ability to hold out a vision of how things could be better. True leadership raises people's sights to a bigger picture and points to what is possible. One of the big difficulties in leadership today is that we are mistaking managing with leadership and vision.

There is a false belief that the statements we have on workplace walls will motivate people to certain behaviour.

In my years in teaching I have seen a huge amount of time put into drawing up wonderful wordy statements of mission. Hours are spent getting the right words, dotting the i's and crossing the t's.

Mission statements

Compelling and attractive mission statements cannot be imposed on people. Putting these on wall plaques does not allow people have ownership of them. Often the vision statement is at odds with what the people experience in their day to day work.

A key question for leaders is to ask whether the espoused values actually match the practice on the ground and if not, what must be done to bring the practice into line with what is espoused.

Rather than wasting time trying to have a common vision leaders would be more effective encouraging individuals who feel passionate about the work to speak to us from the heart about what it is that touches and moves them. Sean Ruth says 'So long as I'm not required to agree with someone else, I can be inspired by them'.[15]

For a moment let me pose this question for you to reflect on. You are in a work situation and there is an opportunity to have new leadership.

What is the first thing that enters your head when you hear of this? We all know that a safe pair of hands is a model many organisations operate out of. Leadership brings change and there is always a fear factor involved.

Leadership and Fear

Leadership brings out painful emotions in people. Sometimes we get scared, confused or feel isolated. Very often when groups are thinking who they would like to elect as their formal leader, they work on a principle-who will allow me continue doing what I am doing without hassling me?

15 Sean Ruth, 2008, Lecture notes, 2013, All Hallows College.

Generally people will not authorise someone to make them face what they don't want to face.

Instead leaders are selected who provide protection and provide stability, someone with solutions that will cause the minimum of disruption.

Leaders are selected to disturb people at a rate they can absorb. This leads to anointing safe leaders and in some organisations a system of musical chairs operates.

There is also a reluctance to allow people make mistakes and learn from them or to allow people develop their own style and approach to leadership. It is as if we are only comfortable with clones of our own style.

The ability to give up control and trust people who have shown they are ready for leadership is a key part of a leadership role. Many of us confuse leadership with authority.

A person can be appointed into a position of authority and have no leadership influence. There are a number of reasons for this.

Authority without leadership

Leadership is an influence relationship rather than an authority. Essentially it's a decision to take initiatives to help things go better.

There are three common reasons why people in authority may not exercise leadership.[16]

1. They have become scared and cut themselves off from others around them. They operate in isolation and do not listen to the thinking of other people.

2. They have too much power and have become divorced from reality experienced by other people.

16 Sean Ruth, Leadership & Liberation 2008, p.35.

3. They have become overwhelmed with administration and paperwork. They literally do not have time to think.

Ruth[17] says we are putting people into formal positions of authority and then making it very difficult, practically, for them to act as leaders.

We are confusing the role of administration with the role of leadership.

It enables us to exercise formal authority, when called on, in ways that are experienced as supportive and liberating.[18]

Leadership and authority

Lead by Example
Encourage from the Heart
Appreciate Diversity
Develop People's Potential
Enable and Empower
Be a **R**ealist
Serve

It is not necessary to be in a formal position of authority to take up a leadership role. There are many people every day with no formal authority who take leadership. Similarly, there are people who have authority but who do not take leadership for one reason or another.

Leadership is a decision we make to see that things work out. By its nature leadership is taken not given. This is a very important statement because many people believe the opposite. There is nothing stopping any one of us taking on leadership roles.

Authority on the other hand is given. It is the right to speak and make decisions for a particular group. Sean Ruth says the more people rely on authority to get things done, the less they do those things that are essentials to real leadership. They become authoritarian rather than leaders.

On the other hand, the more true leadership and authority positions actually do coincide, the less appeal there is to formal authority to get things done. People follow them out of belief in them and commitment to them rather than their position. Leadership is about doing small things well. It is about getting on with activities in life. It's about welding your members into a happy team. It's about having a listening ear for those with problems.

Leadership is

L: Leader

E: Easy

A: Always

D: Doer

E: Enthusiastic

R: Responsible

S: Subtle

H: Helpful

I: Inventive

P: Positive

How to develop leaders

Kanter[19] highlights three important sources of power, that when present enable people to act powerfully. The first is having access to the resources, i.e. money, materials, tools, personnel and so on, that are required to do the job.

The second is access to information, i.e. knowing what is going on, having inside information. The third is access to sup-

19 www.rosabethkanter.com

port i.e. being allowed to exercise initiative and getting support and encouragement from above for this. The more information and support we can provide people with, the more we empower them.

I have made this the central mission of leadership training over the years. Train, provide information and as many resources as possible, hand over and encourage the group of trainees to continue themselves and train others. We have to raise the issue with people of them becoming leaders. We can ask them for help.

We can praise their leadership abilities; we can provide opportunities for them to take up responsible roles. Anything that encourages people to think for themselves is a help to developing leadership. Showing people we believe in them and have a non urgent expectation of them builds confidence to take more leadership responsibility.

We can provide opportunities for training in leadership skills. We can provide opportunities where they experience success. Nowhere does this process criticise the leaders for mistakes made. People can only be encouraged into leadership by people they have a relationship with.

Years ago I heard a very competitive athlete tell a story about climbing a mountain in India. He told us he started at great pace and got half way up the mountain without much hassle. Then he found himself slowing down and watched in amazement as old men walked past him on the climb.

Afterwards he asked one old man what his secret was and he got a reply he said he would never forget: 'You' said the old man 'compete with the mountain.' 'I, on the other hand, let the mountain carry me along.' It is difficult to beat the wisdom. The poem that follows is a great illustration of leadership wisdom:

THE BRIDGE BUILDER[20] - Will Allen Dromgoole

An old man, going a lone highway
Came, at the evening, cold and gray,
To a chasm, vast, and deep and wide,
Through which was flowing a sullen tide.

The old man crossed in the twilight dim;
The sullen stream had no fear for him;
But he turned, when safe on the other side,
And built a bridge to span the tide.

"Old man," said a fellow pilgrim, near,
"You are wasting strength with building here;
Your journey will end with the ending day;
You never again will pass this way;
You've crossed the chasm, deep and wide-
Why build you this bridge at the evening tide?"

The builder lifted his old gray head:
"Good friend, in the path I have come," he said,
"There followeth after me today,
A youth, whose feet must pass this way.

This chasm, that has been naught to me,
To that fair-haired youth may a pitfall be.

He, too, must cross in the twilight dim;
Good friend, I am building this bridge for him."

Obstacle

One of the very subtle obstacles I have experienced is that one is appointed to do a particular task that will bring about change and then given a second job to prevent you doing the first.

---

20 http://www.poetryfoundation.org/poem/237102

This also works by selecting a leader with a vision and then appointing a second person with him or her to stop the vision being implemented.

I heard an old African man saying many years ago 'I am me, I am African.' 'God' he said 'made me- me, and he made you –you.' This idea is beautifully illustrated by Virginia Satir's poem.[21] It is the unique me and you that takes up leadership.

I AM ME!

In all the world,
there is no one else exactly like me -
everything that comes out of me is authentically mine,
because I alone choose it - I own everything about me
- my body, my feelings, my mouth, my voice, all my
actions, whether they be to others or to myself

I own my fantasies, my dreams, my hopes, my fears -
I own all my triumphs and successes, all my failures and
mistakes. Because I own all of me, I can become inti-
mately acquainted with me - by so doing I can love me
and be friendly with me in all my parts -

I know there are aspects about myself that puzzle me,
and other aspects that I do not know -
but as long as I am friendly and loving to myself,
I can courageously and hopefully look for solutions to
the puzzles and for ways to find out more about me -
However I look and sound, whatever I say and do, and
whatever I think and feel at a given moment in time is
authentically me - If later some parts of how I looked,
sounded, thought and felt turned out to be unfitting, I
can discard that which I feel is unfitting, keep the rest,
and invent something new for that which I discarded -
I can see, hear, feel, think, say and do.

21 *I am me* - by Virginia Satir, *www.debradavis.org/gecpage/iamme*.

I have the tools to survive, to be close to others, to be productive,
and to make sense and order out of the world of people and things outside of me -
I own me, and therefore I can engineer me -
I am me & I AM OKAY .

Author: Virginia Satir

When I am looking at leaders I admire I see characteristics of self belief, positivity and wisdom.

We bring ourselves to leadership. We bring our own uniqueness as the poem illustrates. Because 'I am me' I can make choices about life and leadership.

The Leadership Challenge

James Kouzes and Barry Posner developed a survey (The Leadership Practices Inventory)[22] that asked people which of a list of common characteristics of leaders, were, in their experiences of being led by others, the seven top things they look for, admire and would willingly follow. And over twenty years, they managed ask this of seventy five thousand people.

The results of the study showed that people preferred the following characteristics, in order:

> Honest
> Forward-looking
> Competent
> Inspiring
> Intelligent
> Fair-minded
> Broad-minded

22 James Kouzes and Barry Posner developed a survey The Leadership Practices Inventory www.leadershipchallenge.com/about.aspx

> Supportive
> Straightforward
> Dependable
> Cooperative
> Determined
> Imaginative
> Ambitious
> Courageous
> Caring
> Mature
> Loyal
> Self-controlled
> Independent

People act best of all when they are passionate about what they are doing. Leaders unleash the enthusiasm of their followers this with stories and passions of their own. As Paulo Freire[23] put it:

"A leader is not the one who does everything. A leader is the one who makes it possible for others to do."

Chapter Five

The gleanings and sweepings of leadership

Chapter five offers a collection of reflections on diverse notions in leadership. I give copies of these to participants on training workshops. They present ideas on positive thinking, being effective as a leader, the elements of empowerment, bringing out the best in others and humorous ways of looking at leadership.

TALENTED EMPLOYEE[1]

A salesman dropped in to see a business customer. Not a soul was in the office except a big dog emptying wastebaskets. The salesman stared at the animal, wondering if his imagination could be playing tricks on him.

The dog looked up and said "Don't be surprised.

This is just part of my job." "Incredible!" Exclaimed the man.

"I can't believe it! Does your boss know what a prize he has in you? An animal that can talk!" "No, no," pleaded the dog. "Please don't tell him! If that man finds out I can talk, he'll make me answer the phone as well!"

One of the first things I say to people on leadership workshops is that nothing in life is impossible.

The word **IMPOSSIBLE,** I tell them, is made up of

I AM POSSIBLE.

I follow this with the exercise 'What gives you 100% success in life?'

(A) What really makes up 100% in **life**?[2]

Often our language shapes our lives – So if we take the alphabet A through to Z and apply a number to each letter namely 1-26 i.e. there being 26 letters in the English alphabet so, for example, A=1, B=2 and so on.

With that logic in place the following is conceivable:

If Leadership = L+E+A+D+E+R+S+H+I+P

=12+5+1+4+5+18+19+8+9+16 = **97%**

Then H+A+R+D+W+O+R+K

= 8+1+18+4+23+15+18+11 = **98%**

Knowledge would be K+N+O+W+L+E+D+G+E

= 11+14+15+23+12+5+4+7+5 = 96%

And Love would be L+O+V+E

=12+15+22+5=54%

While the sum of Luck would be L+U+C+K

= 12+21+3+11 = 47%

(And yet none of them makes 100%)

So Then what makes 100%?

Is it Money? ….. No!

Is it Happiness? ……. No!

Therefore every problem has a solution, ONLY if we perhaps change our "ATTITUDE". It is OUR ATTITUDE towards life and work that makes OUR life 100% successful.

A+T+T+I+T+U+D+E = 1+20+20+9+20+21+4+5 = 100

Right attitude is vital for leadership.

(B) A Bill of rights for leaders & followers[3]

We, who lead and follow, hold these truths to be self-evident:

THAT every leader is sometimes a follower and every follower is sometimes a leader

THAT the leader leads only when others follow; therefore it is the followers who bestow leadership

THAT, therefore, the power of the leader emanates from the followers

---

3 The grammar of right living - Inspirational Quote Magazine: An Ideal iquote.in/quote_article_detail.php?item_

THAT the collective wisdom of the followers is greater than the individual wisdom of the leader; therefore the leader is called to unleash the wisdom of the whole

THAT since power and wisdom reside in the followers, the leader's goal is to help each follower attain his or her own full potential

THAT the inclination to follow stems from the spirit of the followers and their belief in the integrity of the leader

THAT the leader's goals are viable only when they are held commonly by the followers

THAT all leaders and followers are engaged in a common search to find a sense of individual dignity and worth. Not only do we see these to be self-evident truths, but we hold them to be a BILL of RIGHTS for followers. They are what we expect from each other while being led.

Source: *Gene Denk*

(C) You and your boss[4]

When you take a long time, you're slow.
When your boss takes a long time, he's thorough.
When you don't do it, you're lazy.
When your boss doesn't do it, he's too busy.
When you make a mistake, you're an idiot.
When your boss makes a mistake, he's only human.
When doing something without being told,
You're over-stepping your authority.
When your boss does the same thing,
That's initiative.

---

4 www.begent.org/boss. Also www.boredstupid.com/office_lists/differences_between_you_boss.

When you take a stand, you're being pig-headed.

When your boss does it, he's being firm.

When you overlooked a rule of etiquette, you're being rude.

When your boss skips a few rules, he's being original.

When you please your boss, you're ass-kissing.

When your boss pleases his boss, he's being co-operative.

When you're out of the office, you're wandering around.

When your boss is out of the office, he's on business.

When you're on a day off sick, you're always sick.

When your boss has a day off sick, he must be very ill.

When you apply for leave, you must be going for an interview.

When your boss applies for leave, it's because he's overworked.

(D) 7 ways for leaders to send out a powerful and positive message[5]

1. Leaders manage the process, but lead people

2. Leaders inspire people, they don't just drive them

3. Leaders are easy to respect and look up to

4. Leaders are easy to like and get along with

5. Leaders help people to like themselves

6. Leaders help people to believe that what they're doing is important

7. Leaders are responsive to people

5   Frames: Leadership - Bright Quotes, www.brightquotes.com/lea_fr.

(E) Seven building blocks of collaboration[6]

1. Reinvent yourself as a lateral leader
2. Seek out competent people and strategic partners
3. Build a shared understood goal
4. Designate clear roles and responsibilities, but not restrictive controls or boundaries
5. Spend lots of time in dialogue grounded in real problems
6. Create shared work spaces
7. Load the project with "zest factors"

Mastering the Art of Creative Collaboration, Robert Hargrove

(F) Leadership Characteristics[7]

1. Visionary
2. Integrity
3. Consistency
4. Coach/Facilitator
5. Accessibility
6. Flexibility
7. Courage
8. Over-Communicates
9. Positive Role Model
10. Inspirational

---

6   ibid
7   Frames: Leadership - Bright Quotes, www.brightquotes.com/lea from "Everyone's a Coach" by Don Shula and Ken Blanchard Leadership Characteristics.

(G) Top ten sayings of ineffective leadership [8]

TEN: We don't do it that way around here.

NINE: I don't care what they told you in that training class, this is the real world.

EIGHT: Drop what you are doing and get this to me ASAP!

SEVEN: Don't worry about WHY, just do it!

SIX: Don't let me influence your decisions but here's my opinion.

FIVE: I want you to take risks but remember our motto: "Do it right the first time!"

FOUR: You're planning to work this weekend, aren't you?

THREE: You ought to want to do this.

TWO: We need teamwork. By the way, I'll be doing your individual rankings this week.

ONE: If and when I want your opinion, I'll give it to you.

Empowering others is essentially the process of turning followers into leaders. Empowerment is the process of increasing an individual's belief in his or her effectiveness.

(H) Three keys to Empowerment[9]

1. Sharing Information with Everyone
> Without Information, People cannot Act Responsibly
> With Information, People cannot help but Act responsibly

8 www.n2growth.com/blog/6-traits-of-ineffective-leaders
9 Ken Blanchard, John P. Carlos, Alan Randolph , Release the Power, 1999.

2. Declaring Boundaries that Create Autonomy

> Purpose, Values, Image, Goals, Roles, Structure & Systems. Being Empowered to Act also means you are Accountable for Results.

3. Allow Teams to Self-Manage by: providing training, support and encouragement.

> By encouraging diversity and appreciating individual differences.

-Ken Blanchard

11 Rules on "HOW TO LOSE"[10]

1. Stop taking risks
2. Be content
3. Never deviate from what the founder did
4. Be inflexible
5. Rely totally on research and experts
6. Concentrate on competitors instead of your customers
7. Put yourself - not the customer - first
8. Solve administrative concerns first
9. Let others do your thinking for example, headquarters
10. Rely on T-G-E: "That's Good Enough" and T-N-M-J: "That's Not My Job!"
11. Rationalise slow growth

"It is a curious thing, but perhaps those who are best suited to power are those who have never sought it. Those who, like you, have leadership thrust upon them and take up the mantle because they must, and find to their own surprise that they wear it well." Don Keogh's (CEO Coca-Cola)

---

10 https://www.helpscout.net/.../don-keoghs-ceo-coca-cola-11-rules-on-ho, Don Keogh's (CEO Coca-Cola) 11 Rules on "HOW TO LOSE

(J) Team talk[11]

> If anything goes bad; say "I did it."

> If anything goes semi-good; say "We did it."

> If anything goes real good; say "You did it."

> If you want your team to be a "winner", the above is all that is required.

(K) How to bring out the best in others[12]

1. Ask your people to share their ideas
2. Welcome change
3. Set challenging goals and measure performance
4. Be generous with feedback
5. Reward initiative
6. Develop people who show special potential

(L) In Bill Gates' book Business the Speed of Thought[13]

He allegedly lays out 11 rules that students do not learn in high school or college, but should. He argues that our feel-good, politically correct teachings have created a generation of kids with no concept of reality who are set up for failure in the real world.

RULE 1: Life is not fair; get used to it!

RULE 2: The world won't care about your self-esteem. The world will expect you to accomplish something BEFORE you feel good about yourself.

11 http://quotationsbook.com/quote/31830/
12 Managing Yourself: Bringing Out the Best in Your People - Harvard... hbr.org/2010/05/... yourself-bringing-out-the-best-in-your-people
13 www.truthorfiction.com/rumors/b/billgatesspeech.htm

RULE 3: You will NOT make 40 thousand dollars a year right out of high school. You won't be a vice-president with a car phone, until you earn both a high school and college degree.

RULE 4: If you think your teacher is tough, wait till you get a boss. He doesn't have tenure.

RULE 5: Flipping burgers is not beneath your dignity. Your Grandparents had a different word for burger flipping, they called it opportunity.

RULE 6: If you mess up, it's not your parents' fault, so don't whine about your mistakes, learn from them.

RULE 7: Before you were born, your parents weren't as boring as they are now. They got that way from paying your bills, cleaning your clothes and listening to you talk about how cool you are. So before you save the rain forest from the parasites of your parents' generation, try "delousing" the clothes in your own room.

RULE 8: Your school may have done away with winners and losers but life has not.

RULE 9: Life is not divided into semesters. You don't get summers off and very few employers are interested in helping you FIND YOURSELF. Do that on your own time.

RULE 10: Television is NOT real life. In real life people actually have to leave the coffee shop and go to jobs.

RULE 11: Be nice to nerds. Chances are you'll end up working for one.

(M) How to respond to a rejection letter[14]

The next time you get a rejection letter from a hoped-for employer, just send them the following announcement:

To Whom It May Concern:

Thank you for your letter of [date]. After careful consideration, I regret to inform you that *I am unable to accept your refusal to offer me employment at this time.*

This year I have been particularly fortunate in receiving an unusually large number of rejection letters. With such a varied and promising field of candidates, it is impossible for me to accept all refusals.

Despite [your Company]'s outstanding qualifications and previous experience in rejecting applicants, I find that *your rejection does not meet with my needs at this time.* Therefore, I will initiate employment with your firm immediately. I look forward to working with you.

Best of luck in rejecting future candidates.

Yours.

---

14 Rejection Letter Rebuttal - 48days, 48days.faithsite.com/content.asp?CID=1583 and http://vasantkothari.com/BeyondCampus/?p=58

(N) Yes and No[15]

The No person is always part of the problem

The Yes person is always part of the solution

The No person always has an excuse

The Yes person always has a programme

A No person sees a problem in every answer

A Yes person finds an answer in every problem

A No person says 'Nobody knows'

A Yes person says 'Let's find out'

A No person says 'It may be possible but it's too difficult'

A Yes person says 'It may be difficult but it is possible'

The No person says 'That's the way it always has been done here'

The Yes person says 'Let's keep looking for a better way of doing it'

The No person says 'I am not as bad as a lot of other people'

The Yes person says 'I am good but not as good as I ought to be'

When a No person makes a mistake they say 'it wasn't my fault'

When a Yes person makes a mistake they say 'I am sorry, I was wrong'

The No person tries to tear down those who are superior to them

15 Author unknown.

The Yes person tries to learn from those who are superior to them

A No person makes promises

A Yes person makes commitments

(Author unknown)

(O)　Gardening guide for Leaders[16]

First plant four rows of peas:
> The peas stand for preparedness, perseverance, politeness and prayer.

Next to them plant three rows of squash:
> Squash gossip, squash criticism, squash indifference.

> Then put five rows of Lettuce:

> Let us be faithful, let us be loyal and let us be selfless,

> let us be truth & let us love one another

> Finally remember no veggie garden is complete without turnips

Turn up for meetings, turn up with a smile, turn up with a new idea, turn up determined to make the new week better than the last.

---

16 www.realworlduniversity.com/?p=369, planting your spiritual garden

Chapter Six

Theories of Leadership

In examining leadership one must look at various theories. Chapter six presents you with basic information on the following theories:

The lone leader, trait leader, classic leader situational and participative leadership. You will also find short explanations on behavioural theory and power.

In the beginning, corporate style[1]

In the Beginning, there was **The Plan** but The Plan was without form and man created **The Procedure**. Darkness was upon the face of the employees and they were so afraid; and they looked upon their supervisors and cried "It is a crock of dung and stinks to High Heaven!"

1   www.rare-leadership.org/humor_on_work-business-leadership-success.ht...

And the supervisors spoke unto the project supervisors, saying "It is a bucket of manure and intolerably malodorous."

And the project administrators spoke unto the section managers, saying "It is a vessel of fertilizer and exceedingly strong."

And the section managers spoke unto the department directors, saying "It promoteth growth and is very powerful."

And the department directors spoke unto the company president, saying "It augmenteth development and productivity."

And the company president looked down on The Procedure and declared "AND IT WAS GOOD!"

And so the Plan became Policy. This is how *Shit Happens*.

Leadership is the influencing, motivating, guiding, directing or coordinating of individuals, groups, communities or organisations in a way that affects their behaviour or actions, especially in relation to bringing about change .

There is a need for some gifted individuals who understand what leadership involves and are willing to put themselves forward or accept the role if they are asked by a group. There is need for an appropriate framework within which leadership and authority is exercised. The possibility of good leadership is affected by the views and attitudes of the people the leader is asked to lead.

We speak of different types of leaders and sometimes get caught up in applying a particular theory while failing to see that people are bigger than a theory. The theory gives us indications but it is not the full picture.

The lone leader is a person, like the Buddha, with a personal vision who sets out to follow it with little intention of trying to lead others. Many people are inspired by their single mindedness and gather around to become followers of this person. Leaders like this focus on following their own star.

This kind of leader will follow a purpose because it is worthwhile and are not interested in influencing others. Covey says the first stage of leadership is finding one's own voice. Leaders need to know what they believe in. They need to have a personal vision and the discipline to stand up for the truths and values which give meaning to their lives.[2]

Trait Theory[3]

Great man theories assume that the capacity for leadership is inherent – that great leaders are born not made.[4] The term "Great Man" was used because at the time leadership was thought of primarily as a male quality, especially in terms of military leadership.

Many believe certain personal qualities make good leaders.

Maybe they have strong personalities or they are able to inspire people when they speak or they have a vision which makes people want to follow them. The trait theory assumes that people inherit certain qualities and traits that make them better suited to leadership.

These traits include ability, intelligence, originality, good judgement, being well qualified, having a sense of responsibility, energy and drive, a willingness to take risks and to organise others.

2   7 Habits of Highly Effective People - Habit ... - Stephen Covey
3   RG Lord, CL De Vader, GM Alliger - Journal of Applied Psychology, 1986 - psycnet.apa.org
4   From article based on a chapter of a book by Edwin A. Locke, Shelley A. Kirkpatrick, Jill K. Wheeler, Jodi Schneider, Kathryn Niles, Harold Goldstein, Kurt Welsh, & Dong-OK Chah, entitled The Essence of Leadership. http://amp.aom.org/content/5/2/48.short

There is a danger if this theory is taken too far as it suggests the leaders are larger than life, visionary; and they are like supermen, saviours and heroes. Masculine strengths are seen but feminine qualities are often ignored.

The classic leader

The classic leader has a personal vision but it cannot be realised without the involvement of others. Nelson Mandela[5] was a good example of this type of leader. He wanted to bring about change in South Africa and inspire others to do so. In the Long road to freedom, Mandela says

'I have walked that long road to freedom. I have tried not to falter; I have made missteps along the way. But I have discovered the secret that after climbing a great hill, one only finds that there are many more hills to climb.

I have taken a moment here to rest, to steal a view of the glorious vista that surrounds me, to look back on the distance I have come. But I can rest only for a moment, for with freedom comes responsibilities, and I dare not linger, for my long walk is not yet ended'.[6]

The aim of the classic leader is to inspire others. He or she relates well to others, gives rousing speeches, writes well and organises rousing rallies to present the message.

Classic leadership involves a projection of energy which draws others into the vision of the leader and involves transformation of a situation as the leader sees it.

In Nelson Mandela's situation it meant the dismantling of the Apartheid system.

---

5   Knowledge Management: Classic and Contemporary Works Edited by Daryl Morey, Mark T. Maybury, Bhavani M. Thuraisingham,
6   'Long Road to Freedom' Nelson Mandela http://www.scu.edu/ethics/architects-of-peace/Mandela/essay.html p.751.

Behavioural Theory[7]

The Behavioural theory of leadership is the opposite of the trait theory. It is based upon the belief that great leaders are made, not born. Rooted in behaviourism, this leadership theory focuses on the actions of leaders not on mental qualities or internal states. According to this theory, people can learn to become leaders through teaching and observation. This theory[8] suggests that certain behavioural patterns may be identified as leadership styles.

Applications of behavioural theory promote the value of leadership styles with an emphasis on concern for people and participative decision making, encouraging collaboration and team development by supporting individual needs and aligning individual and group objectives.

Situational Theories[9]

Situational theories propose that leaders choose the best course of action based upon situational variables. It proposes that the effectiveness of a particular style of leadership is dependent on the context in which it is being exercised. From situation to situation, different styles may be more appropriate for certain types of decision making.[10]

According to situational leadership, different people can be successful in different circumstances. The successful leader will be the person with the qualities suited to the situation. There is no one best way. Leadership styles can fall along a range of control.

7 ibid
8 Leadership theories, Business balls, http://www.businessballs.com/leadership-theories.htm
   And Toward a behavioural theory of charismatic leadership in organizational settings, JA
   Conger, RN Kananga - Academy of Management Review, 1987.
9 Small bizconnect-, understanding leadership. http://toolkit.smallbiz.nsw.gov.au/
   part/8/38/185-article
10 ibid

At one end it might be autocratic and the other end, it might be democratic. The autocratic often rely on rules and procedures, while the democratic prefer shared planning and responsibility.

The autocratic assume their status should be respected while the democratic rely on performance rather than status to win respect. The situational approach shows that leadership involves more than personal traits. It also involves dealing with people in actual situations and it's possible that leaders may change their styles depending on the situation.

There is a danger with this theory if taken too far: the situational approach emphasises doing things right for the circumstances.

Some people argue that you can be manipulated by a leader who changes style to get what he/she wants. Good leadership goes beyond technique or behaviour and involves morals and values.

Management Theories[11]

Management theories, also known as transactional theories, focus on the role of supervision, organisation and group performance. These theories base leadership on a system of rewards and punishments. Managerial theories are often used in business when employees are successful, they are rewarded; when they fail, they are reprimanded or punished.

Participative Theories[12]

Participative leadership theories suggest that the ideal leadership style is one that takes the input of others into account.

11 Organisational Behaviour, Angeelo, Kinicki, 2008
12 http://psychology.about.com/od/leadership/p/leadtheories.htm

These leaders encourage participation and contributions from group members and help group members feel more relevant and committed to the decision-making process.

In participative theories, however, the leader retains the right to allow the input of others. In this type of management, employees at all levels are encouraged to contribute ideas towards identifying and setting organisational-goals, problem solving and other decisions that may directly affect them. It is also called consultative management.[13]

Relationship Theories[14]

Relationship theories, also known as transformational theories, focus upon the connections formed between leaders and followers.

Transformational leaders motivate and inspire people by helping group members see the importance and higher good of the task.

These leaders are focused on the performance of group members, but also want each person to fulfil his or her potential.

Leaders with this style often have high ethical and moral standards.

Transformational Leadership

Studies by Meyer and Allen[15] show that people working under a charismatic leader report greater job satisfaction than those under more traditional or structural leadership.

It is important to note that charisma is not equal to leadership.

13 http://www.businessdictionary.com/definition/participative-management.html#ixzz2uFMt-nnE6
14 ibid
15 managementstudyguide.com/participative-management.

Neither is charisma necessary or efficient to cause leadership. However, charismatic leadership is the strongest factor in transformational leadership.[16]

Bolman and Deal[17] make a very telling comment about leadership. They say leaders make things happen, but things also make leaders happen. What worked 30 years ago will not work today. It takes a different type of person.

Transformational leaders define the need for change.

They create commitment to the vision and concentrate on long-term goals. They also inspire others to transcend personal interests, change the organisation to accommodate vision.

Leaders need mentoring. Key behaviours of transformational leaders include creating a common vision, building trust and empowering others.[18]

Leadership is about power[19]

In this theory people argue if you want to understand leadership, you must understand power relationships in society. People who are appointed as leaders have a formal power; they may use this negatively, i.e. enriching themselves or positively, by working for the good of others.

There is a difference between power and authority. Someone has power if they are able to get others to do what they want by persuading or by using force.

A person has authority if they hold power legitimately, that is, if they are formally appointed to a position. If they earn the respect of others, they have personally earned authority. In a democratic society the other side of power is accountability.

---

16 Maddock & Fulton, Motivation, Emotion & Leadership, 1998
17 Bolman and Deal, Reframing Organizations 2009, p 344
18 Maddock & Fulton , Motivation, Emotion & Leadership, 1998
19 Leadership and Ethics, with purposeful actions, pdf, training manual

Gender relations are an important set of power in society. Power is defined as the ability and desire to control but power alone does not make good leadership.

Power can, however, contribute to effective leadership by enabling the leader to take necessary steps to create change. It can allow a leader to guide even through fear and intimidation. But power alone cannot yield purposeful leadership.[20]

Group leadership[21]

Group leadership involves more than one person. Leadership often exists through a group of people working together closely. In a school we have year heads and department heads as examples of this. By broadening your theory of leadership you will see that leaders don't have to do everything themselves.

They must make sure that the group as a whole sets goals and has a vision. Delegation and responsibility are two important factors in this. Delegation is passing power on to other people. Delegated members must have a clear understanding of what is expected of them.

Group leadership is the process of providing focus and direction to a specific group of people. Leadership of this type often involves facilitating and guiding the actions of group participants as well as accepting responsibility for the outcome of the group's efforts.[22]

John Adair's[23] Action-Centred Leadership model provides a great blueprint for leadership and the management of any team, group or organisation.

20 Bass Bernard M., Bass, Ruth, 2009, The Bass Handbook of Leadership: Theory, Research, and Managerial Applications
21 Ingrid Bens 2006. Facilitating to Lead. Jossey-Bass
22 Wisegeek.com
23 www.learn-to-be-a-leader.com/john-adair.

He suggests ten points for building a leadership team.

Ten points plan for your team[24]

1. Each member has something to add to your team.
2. Formulate team objectives carefully and always take them seriously.
3. Remember that team members must support each other.
4. Break long term aims into short term projects.
5. Try forming bonds with other team members.
6. Remind members that they are team participants.
7. Make use of the great power of friendship to strengthen the team.
8. Look for strong team commitment from a leader.
9. Always reward merit but never let errors go unnoticed.
10. Remember that everyone in a team thinks in a different way.

24 http://www.teambuilding.co.uk/john-adair-team-theory.html

Chapter Seven

Types of allegorical non-human leadership

This chapter focuses on allegorical non-human models of leadership.

Kipper Leadership[1]

Over the years doing leadership workshops I have always carried a bag of magnetic fish. At the end of the training I give each participant one to take away and a parting comment that fish rot from the head down. Fish might unfairly be accused of being two-faced, as you only get to see one side at once.

This principle is also applicable to the two-faced leader who has different faces and styles depending on the situation. I once heard an African politician describing himself as a Chameleon.

1 http://changingminds.org/disciplines/leadership/articles/kippermanagement.htm

A Chameleon changes his colour depending on the situation to blends in. The kipper will change with the wind as the need arises. They are your friends when things need doing and back-stabbers when there is glory or reward to be gained. The kipper's hero is probably Machiavelli.

Why it happens

The key reason why the kipper is so two-faced (or many-faced) is that their values with regard to integrity are largely non-existent. They literally see nothing wrong in acting differently with different people and may even be proud of their ability to act differently in different situations, calling it something like 'style flexibility'.

What to do about it

Make sure you always have something that the kipper needs. This will keep their kinder face towards you. If the kipper regularly turns their bad face on you, consider fighting fire with fire and standing up to them.

Many kippers will turn a kinder face to those who are not easily cowed. Also consider taking the matter further, particularly if you can show the kipper is seriously breaking company values.

Kippers are natural cowards and admire power. They are hence susceptible to blackmail, although this is seldom a good approach. If, however, they know that you know something that they do not want others to know, no words may be necessary and they may treat you much better.

The kipper may also happily betray themselves in boasts of what and how they got people to do things for them.

Mushroom leadership[2]

Mushroom is a common metaphor in leadership and management. The 'mushroom leader' plants you knee-deep (or worse) in the smelly stuff and keeps you in the dark.

In practice, this means you get to do all the work that they do not want.

They do not communicate and generally ignore you, so you do not know their plans or what else might be going on.

Why it happens

Mushroom leaders are often more concerned about their own career and image. Anyone who appears as a threat may well be deliberately held back as their ability may make the mushroom leader look bad.

Mushroom leaders may also have their favourites on whom they lavish attention and the plum jobs.

Others are swept away and given the dregs. Sometimes mushroom leaders are just incompetent and know no better.

What to do about it

Be assertive.

Talk to them about what they are doing and the effect they are having.

Do not lie down and be the doormat who says 'thank you' for any scraps they care to throw you.

Remember that you always have more <u>power</u> than you think you have.

Take up your own leadership.

2 http://changingminds.org/disciplines/leadership/articles/mushroommanagementt.htm

Seagull Leadership/management[3]

'Seagull leadership/ management' is a humorous term that is used to describe a style of leadership whereby the person 'flies in, poops on you and then flies away again'.

When they are there, they typically give criticism and direction in equal quantities, often without any real understanding of what the job entails. Then before you can object or ask what they really want, they have an 'important meeting' to go to. Whilst they are there, they talk non-stop and actively discourage anyone else from saying anything.

This can include avoiding eye contact and continuing to talk over you if you start to say anything.

Why it happens

The Seagull leader likes to consider themselves as important. However they also know that they do not know that much and fear being exposed by questions or debate.

They consequently talk at you and do not stop until they can excuse themselves and leave. Their approach is transactional, based on the simple premise 'do as I say and you'll continue to get paid'.

What to do about it

What you need to do about Seagull Managers depends largely on your job. If you can work independently, then the best approach is often to listen patiently then ignore them. As long as you are delivering value, they may not actually be too concerned about how you get there.

Generally they are not that interested in control over you.

3   http://changingminds.org/disciplines/leadership/articles/seagulmanagement.htm

I've discovered that if you approach a Seagull leader with complex details and facts and figures, they will withdraw from you because the most important thing in the Seagull leader's life is the Seagull leader.

If you can deliver results, then they may well leave you to your own devices or give moderate support.

Animal leadership

Over my years in Africa I have spent time observing animals in the wild. I have learnt a lot about leadership as a result. Observe a herd of elephants, a pride of lions, a troop of monkeys or a swarm of bees.

Who assumes leadership? The examples of animal leadership can be used to inform how you define leadership.

The Lion

Observe a pride of lions. A dominant/alpha male is the leader of this group. None can challenge the strength of the alpha male. The physical strength and aggression of the alpha male is the determining factor of his dominance. The protection and security enjoyed by other members of the pride at the behest of the alpha lion is what keeps the pride together.

But the leadership of the alpha male is always under threat. During breeding season, the dominant male lions from other pride challenge the leadership domain and some time may win also.

Once it wins, the new one takes control of the entire pride. It kills all the cubs of the previous leader to establish authority. This pushes the females into heat so he can have his mating. Leadership of the dominant lion in a pride is not stable and inspirational.

Mere physical strength is what defines the leadership Similar to this; some leaders in a business behave exactly the same way as the new lion chief of the pride. They often bring in their own people.

The Elephant

In the case of an elephant herd, the matured and elderly female is the head. The headship is less challenged, the constant guidance and inspiration is the key determining factor of her dominance in the herd.

When the matriarchal head loses its head to old age, the next aged one is unanimously selected as the team head. The survival of the entire herd is depending on the experienced guidance of the aged female. The aged female elephant never acts like a boss but has solutions to the herd's problems.

Using the Elephant style, take the people with the greatest experience and place them at the helm for stability, reassurance and reflection. A few younger, quick-witted leaders can be sourced for advice but the one stable leader at the top should hold gentle sway.

The emphasis is on the wisdom leader figure which in many cases in the western world gets discarded. In the African culture the elder carries great leadership and respect.

The Bee

Again, from observation the leadership of the bee is very interesting. Here the queen (leader) remains only for the purpose of procreation. Different bees are entrusted with different responsibilities. There is no conflict in the division of labour. It is highly organised and very systematic.

When the queen dies, a new queen is developed by the rest of the members. In the swarm of bees, only one queen is entertained. We need to look at the positive and negative if we are to improve our leadership skills.

Animals show in a clear way some kind of human behaviour. Consider your own leadership looking at the following creatures.

Being an animal

Training leaders involves transformation. I use 'Being an animal' in a fun way in training.

I break the group into partners and get them to ask "Are there other kinds of animals around in groups?" and let people describe their characteristics if they can suggest ones not listed.

You can also brainstorm 'What kinds of animals and their characteristics would you like to see in groups?' turning it into a positive. I ask if a leader was one of these creatures what their style of leadership would be. I also use it to look at notions of stereotypes. For instance a mouse is not "too timid to speak up on any subject".

I often end the session by inviting trainees to make the sounds of 'their' animal.

Unhelpful behaviour in leadership training groups[4]

> **The Donkey** is very stubborn and will not change his/her point of view.

> **The Lion** gets into fights whenever others disagree with his/her plans or interferes with his/ her decisions.

4 Taken from 'Unhelpful behaviour in a group; Animal codes' beginning on page 71 of Book 2 of Training for Transformation - a handbook for community workers by Anne Hope and Sally Timmel, Mambo Press, 1984

> **The Rabbit** runs away as soon as he/she sense tension or conflict. It's called flight behaviour.

> **The Ostrich** buries his/ her head in the sand and refuses to face reality or admit there is a problem at all. The problem with this style of leadership is you can get kicked in the ass when your head is buried and you have no idea who did the kicking.

> **The Frog** croaks on and on about the same subject in a monotonous tone.

> The Hippo who sleeps a lot and only puts up his head from the water to yawn.

> **The Cat** always looking for sympathy. 'It's so difficult for me'. Miaow!

> **The Fish** who sits there with a cold glassy stare, not responding to anyone or anything.

> **The Chameleon** who changes colour according to the people she is with. She'll say one thing to this group and something else to another.

> **The Snake** hides in the grass and strikes unexpectedly.

> **The Owl** looks very solemn and pretends to be always talking in long words and complicated sentences.

> **The Peacock** who is always showing off, competing for attention. Saying to us 'Look at what a fine fellow I am'!

> **The Rhino** who charges around, head down, upsetting people unnecessarily and always putting his/her feet in it.

> **The Mouse** who is too timid to say anything on any subject.

> **The Elephant** who stubbornly blocks the way and prevents the group continuing along the road to a desired goal.

> **The Tortoise** who withdraws from the group and refuses to give his/ her opinions or ideas.

> **The Giraffe** who looks down on others, and the programme in general, feeling "I am above all this childish nonsense."

> **The Monkey** who fools around, chattering away, preventing the group from concentrating on any serious business.

In the next chapter inspired leadership will be looked at.

Chapter Eight

Inspired Leadership

The following stories are concerned with quick thinking in awkward situations!

SURPRISE VISIT[1]

Resolving to surprise her husband, an executive's wife stopped by his office. She found him with his secretary sitting in his lap. Without hesitating, he dictated "...and in conclusion, gentlemen, shortage or no shortage, I cannot continue to operate this office with just one chair."

The shredding machine[2]

A young executive was leaving the office late one evening when he found the CEO standing in front of a shredder with

1   http://www.jokes99.com/joke/64
2   www.digitaldreamdoor.com/pages/quotes/business

a piece of paper in his hand. "Listen," said the CEO, "this is a very sensitive and important document here and my secretary has gone for the night. Can you make this thing work?". "Certainly," said the young executive, eager to be perceived as helpful. He turned the machine on, inserted the paper, and pressed the start button. "Excellent, excellent!" said the CEO as his paper disappeared inside the machine. "I just need one copy."

We follow leaders who inspire us. But what makes a leader inspiring? This chapter examines the central characteristics necessary for inspiration.

The Quiet Leader[3]

The actions of a leader speak louder than his or her words. People are motivated when you give them credit rather than take it yourself.

The approach of quiet leaders is the antithesis of the classic charismatic (and often transformational) leaders in that they base their success not on ego and force of character but on their thoughts and actions.

They are strongly task-focused and persuade people through rational argument and a form of benevolent Transactional Leadership.

The 'Level 5' leader[4]

In his book Good to Great, Jim Collins, identified five levels of effectiveness people can take in organisations. At level four is the merely effective leader, whilst at level five is the leader who combines professional will with personal humility.

3   ibid- Leadership quotes
4   Jim Collins, pdf 'Where are you on your journey, from good to great,' www.jimcollins.com/tools/diagnostic-tool

The 'professional will' indicates how they are far from being timid wilting flowers and will march against any advice if they believe it is the right thing to do. In 'personal humility' they put the well-being of others before their own personal needs, for example, giving others credit after successes but taking personal responsibility for failures.

Taoist writings[5]

The quiet leader is not a modern invention and Lao Tzu, who, in the classic Taoist text Tao Te Ching, was discussing the same characteristic around 500 BC:

> The very highest is barely known by men,
>
> Then comes that which they know and love,
>
> Then that, which is feared,
>
> Then that which is despised.
>
> He who does not trust enough will not be trusted.
>
> When actions are performed
>
> Without unnecessary speech,
>
> People say "We did it!"
>
> Here again, the highest level of leadership is virtually invisible.

Leadership which is inspirational[6]

An inspired and motivated team is essential for any business or group that hopes to stay ahead of the competition. But just how do you motivate people? What kind of leadership do people respond to? And how can you improve the quality

5   Ramsey, S. Chenab, 2006 The Art of Leadership
6   http://michaelhyatt.com Helping leader Leverage influence.

of leadership in your business, in your team, your school and your church? Inspirational leaders can motivate people. In the movie Braveheart[7] there is a scene where William Wallace addresses his men

I am William Wallace and I see a whole army of my countrymen, here in defiance of tyranny! You have come to fight as free men and free men you are! What will you do without freedom? Will you fight?"A veteran shouts, "Fight? Against that? No, we will run; and we will live."

Wallace responds: Aye, fight and you may die. Run and you'll live … at least for a while. And dying in your beds, many years from now, would you be willing' to trade all the days, from this day to that, for one chance, just one chance, to come back here and tell our enemies that they may take our lives, but they'll never take … our freedom.

The men are inspired and Wallace leads them into battle. They defeat the British, who were more numerous and better equipped. Later in the movie, Robert the Bruce has a discussion about leadership with his father.

He understands that there is a fundamental difference between having a leadership title and actually being an inspirational leader. Inspirational leaders share four characteristics in common.

> They set a pace.

> Believe in the future.

> Get people to connect with a greater picture in life

> They inspire people to believe in themselves. We have all met such leaders in our life time.

The following are some of the most commonly observed characteristics of inspiring leaders. Jonathan Farrington tells us these are

7   http://forum.uyghuramerican.org/forum/showthread.php?3388-Here-is-the-speech-of-William-Wallace-from-quot-Braveheart-quot

Strong Strategic Focus[8]

They are very good at ensuring that the business only does those things where it has the resources to do a good job and where it can add real value.

Lateral Thinkers[9]

They are particularly adept at drawing on experiences, outside their own and taking a much broader view than the norm.

They look at things very laterally and encourage their people to do the same.

Vision and Communication[10]

An inspirational leader has a very strong, customer-focused vision of where the organisation or business should be going.

Importantly, they are also able to communicate their vision so that their people feel they own it and know where they fit into it.

The best leaders are great communicators who prefer plain speaking to jargon.

Principled[11]

They are deeply committed, courageous, demanding of themselves and their people and confident. What singles them out is an exceptionally strong set of values built on honesty, openness and true respect for their people.

---

8   Jonathan Farrington, 2008. 'Addressing the Inspiration Gap', p.1.
9   ibid p. 1.
10 ibid p. 2.
11 ibid p. 2.

What makes an inspiring leader?[12]

Reflective

Inspirational leaders believe in the future. They are able to paint a vivid picture of a different and better reality. They **make** it concrete, so people can see, imagine and believe. What distinguishes them is genuine humility and not being afraid to show vulnerability on occasions. This comes from regular periods of reflection and always being open to new learning.

Risk Takers[13]

They have a marked tendency to 'bend the rules', take calculated risks and on occasions, be guided by their gut-feelings. They also tolerate this in other people, recognising that a certain amount of flexibility is essential to adapt to circumstances and make real strides forward.

Accessible[14]

They make time to get out and speak to people. This informal and personal contact is a very powerful motivator.

Value Attitude[15]

They value skills and training very highly but they also focus heavily on attitude. They follow the principle that attitude determines your altitude.

12 Are You An Inspirational Leader? Monique Stoner >> www.moniquestoner.com/are-you-an-inspirational-leader
13 https://www.google.ie/#q=++www.moniquestoner.com%2Fare-you-an-inspirational-leader (blog post)
14 https://www.google.ie/#q=++www.moniquestoner.com%2Fare-you-an-inspirational-leader
15 https://www.google.ie/#q=++www.moniquestoner.com%2Fare-you-an-inspirational-leader

SECRETS TO SUCCESS[16]

A reporter asked a bank president, "Sir, What is the secret of your success?"

"Two words: Right decisions."

"And how do you make right decisions?"

"One word: Experience."

"And how do you get experience?"

"Two words: Wrong decisions."

Why people respond to leaders[17]

Being Listened To

Inspirational leaders ask for and respect what their people tell them about how to do things better.

Being Involved

Inspirational leaders involve their people in changes for them to be a success.

Having Fun

In successful companies, people work hard but enjoy themselves in the process. Enjoyment is a great indicator that an organisation is innovative and is also a key innovation driver.

Being Trusted

It's no coincidence that when you ask people what it is like to work in an organisation run by an inspirational leader, they talk about openness, honesty, respect and trust.

16 boardofwisdom.com/Togo/Quotes/ShowQuote?msgid=534636
17 The Art of Inspiring People Athena Tavoulari Stanton Chase, www.stantonchase.com

Being Appreciated

Recognition is an absolutely crucial element of inspiration, and few things are more powerful, or simple, than a genuine 'thank you'.

I had a school headmaster one time who believed in taking the teachers out for a celebration each term. It built a strong team.

In order to have good leadership it is necessary to have 'consistency'. The story of the hare and tortoise is a classic illustration of this.

LEADERSHIP CONSISTENCY

The Story of the Hare and the Tortoise[18]

Would you like to explain the importance of persistence using a story? Sometimes stories are more useful than training games. After you have read the story, ask yourself the question: 'Are you a tortoise or a hare?'

Once there were two friends - a hare and a tortoise. The hare was known for his swiftness and the tortoise was known for his sluggishness. The tortoise was extremely slow.

One day, as they chatted, the hare began making fun of the tortoise for his slowness.

The tortoise was slightly annoyed but said with a smile, "I may be slow, but I can beat you in a race."

The hare was astonished to hear this. He thought the tortoise was utterly foolish and totally unaware of what he could not do, even in his wildest dreams. "Are you kidding?" said the hare in bewilderment. "I hope you are not serious."

18 www.storyarts.org/library/aesops/stories

"I am very serious. I am sure I can outrun you," said the tortoise. Seeing the tortoise so serious, the hare said, "All right, in that case, we shall appoint a referee and fix a venue for the event."

On that note they parted, to meet again on the appointed date. A rat was appointed as referee. A large field beside the river was selected for the unusual race and a big banyan tree, about a mile away from the rat's hole, was decided on to be the winning post.

The rat stood ready to blow the whistle and start the race. The tortoise and the hare tensed at the start line. "On your mark, get set, go", called the rat, and the race began.

The hare took off at lightning speed and soon ran out of sight towards the finish line.

Meanwhile the tortoise began the race at a very slow pace.

The sight was almost funny if not pitiful. "Poor tortoise," thought the rat, "The hare will win the race hands down and cover the length of the field ten times before the tortoise can cover it even once. No match at all!"

The hare must have reached about half a mile when he stopped to see where the tortoise was. He looked back. The tortoise was not to be seen. "Oh he is far behind; I can't even see him yet. I think I will wait here until I can see him and then I'll run the remaining distance. Hey, why don't I eat some grass and rest in the meanwhile." said the hare to himself.

The hare snacked and drank some water, and lay down in the shade of a tree to wait and watch. Soon the cool air from the riverside lulled him into deep sleep. The tortoise, on the other hand, kept moving slowly but steadily. The hare slept for a long time. When he woke up, he felt rested and so decided to complete the race.

He looked around and the tortoise was not to be seen anywhere. As he approached the finish line he grew more and more astonished. The tortoise had already reached the finish line. The hare had lost the race.

He accepted the defeat graciously.

After that he never poked fun at the tortoise or his slowness.

The moral of the story: If you have all that you need to win the race, the only thing that could stop you from winning the race is lack of persistence in effort.

The Lesson

Which one of the two was consistent? The tortoise of course. He believed that it did not matter how tough the goal was, if he kept at it and did a little every moment, he would be able to achieve it.

To win he needed to put in work steadily, even if it was slow. He took time to do all the right things at the right time.

Chapter Nine

A prayer suitable for the work day

Dear Lord, so far today, I've done all right.

I haven't gossiped and I haven't lost my temper. I haven't been grumpy, nasty or selfish and I'm really glad of that!

But in a few minutes, Lord, I'm going to get out of bed and from then on, I'm probably going to need a lot of help.

Thank you! Amen.[1]

Jesus the greatest Leader of all time

In all the leadership programmes I have run I ask the participants to name 5 leaders they admire. I have never been given Jesus as an answer.

There are far too many things to be said about the leadership of Jesus than a chapter in a book could possibly cover. I want to focus on a few of the attributes and skills that Jesus had. These same skills and attributes are important to us if we wish to succeed as leaders.

Ken Blanchard says: 'Effective leadership-whether on the job, in the community, at church or in the home-starts on the inside. Before you can hope to lead anyone else, you have to know who you are.[2]

Jesus' style of relationship

The quality of relationship is central to leadership. It is the measure of authenticity. Looking at Jesus we see he was real. He identified with people, affirmed them, shared decision making and didn't try to change them. He showed how to love people one person at a time. He gave what was wanted by the people and didn't play it safe.

KEY ELEMENTS OF CHRISTIAN LEADERSHIP

Jesus was a listener.

He created a vision.

He was authentic.

He was compassionate.

He was forgiving.

He was straightforward.

He empowered people.

He was a person of integrity.

He was generative.

2   Ken Blanchard (Author), Phil Hodges, Lead like Jesus: Lessons from the Greatest Leadership Role Model of All Time

Fixed principles

Jesus knew who he was and why he was on earth. That meant he could lead from strength rather than from uncertainties. Jesus operated from a base of fixed principles and truths rather than making up the rules as he went along. His leadership style was constant. Those who cling to power at the expense of principle often end up doing almost anything to perpetuate their power.

Jesus said several times 'Come follow me'. He had a programme of 'do what I do' rather than 'do what I say'. He walked and worked closely with those he was to serve. He built relationships with them. He was not afraid of close friendships; he was not afraid that proximity to him would disappoint his followers.

Understanding

Jesus was a listening leader. He listened without condemnation. He loved his followers and he was able to be straight and upfront with them. He reproved Peter at times because he loved him and Peter grew as a result.

Selfless leadership

Jesus was selfless. He put himself second and others first. His leadership emphasised the importance of being discerning with others.

He cared about the freedom of his followers to choose.

His made a choice himself to go to hang on a cross.

He taught there can be no growth without freedom.

By contrast some of the world's leaders today manipulate

their followers and use them. Such leaders focus on their own needs and desires and not on the needs of the people who follow them.

> *"The leader is like a shepherd. He stays behind the flock, letting the most nimble go on ahead, whereas the others follow, normalising all along that they are being directed from behind. There are times when a leader must move out ahead of the flock, go off in a new direction, confident that he is leading his people the right way."*
>
> - Nelson Mandela, *"The Long Walk to Freedom"* [3]

Responsibility

Jesus knew how to involve his disciples in the process of life. He gave them important and specific things to do for their development. Many leaders try to do everything themselves and refuse to delegate.

Jesus trusts his followers enough to share his work with them so that it can grow.

That is one of the great lessons of leadership. If we go it alone, the task may get done but without the growth and development in followers that is important.

One of the messages I've put out to people who attend my courses is the need to develop and trust themselves. I believe in training and handing over and leaving leaders behind me.

Jesus was not afraid to make demands on those he led. He had courage to call Peter and others to leave their fishing nets and follow him, not after the fishing season finished, but right now! Today!

Many leaders are contemptuous of humanity because they treat people as if they were to be molly coddled forever.

3   Nelson Mandela, 1995, Long Walk to Freedom Little Brown & Co

Jesus believed in his followers, not alone for what they were, but for the possibilities to become.

Jesus was a teacher

Jesus communicated his vision clearly to his disciples.

He told them that he had come into the world that the world through him could be saved.

He lived out his vision before the disciples so they knew what it was. Sometimes, they didn't get it. Even at the last supper, there was some confusion as to where Jesus was going and why the disciples couldn't go with him.

A leader must have a clear vision, be focused on accomplishing it and communicate it well to his people. Proverbs 29:18 reminds us that where there is no vision, the people perish.[4]

Jesus was a recruiter

Jesus surrounded himself with men he recruited. He had looked into their hearts and lives and had determined they would be the best he could find. Good leaders need to surround themselves with good people. They should not settle for mediocrity.

Note the characteristics of the 12 disciples: they were loyal, trustworthy, could interact well with people, had enormous skills, were dedicated to the vision and mission of their leader, communicated well with Jesus and the team, worked well in the team, were not self serving and could work independently.

These men were so dedicated to their mission that they were killed fulfilling it. They were singular in following the strategic plan laid out for them.

4 Proverbs 29:18 New Revised Version

Jesus was an authority figure

No matter which translation of the Bible you read, you find Jesus speaking with authority.

When He went head to head with those in authority, He usurped them by answering their question with a question.

He did not become defensive in their presence. He had full authority and He intended to exercise it when necessary. He did the same with His followers. He told them to love their enemies and to do good to those who hated them.

He didn't suggest it. He spoke the truth without apology.

He led by example

Jesus told his Disciples what to be as well as what to do. He encouraged them to be perfect.

Among other things He told them to love, obey, pray, walk, listen and follow.

He was inspirational

In all of Jesus' teachings, there are no rah-rah rallies. There are no pep talks. He motivated and motivates people without the expected tape series, seminars or best-selling books.

He had integrity.

Abraham Lincoln said that "nearly all men can stand adversity but if you want to test a man's character, give him power."

Nothing will motivate your people greater than the knowledge that their leader is a man or woman with integrity, one who cannot and will not be bought, who will die before compromising his or her convictions.

Accountability

Jesus taught us that we are not only accountable for our actions but for our thoughts. This is important to remember. We live in an age that stresses 'no fault'.

I have heard coaches shouting 'no fault' after a blatant miss in a game. Accountability is not possible without fixed principles. A good leader will remember that he is accountable to God as well as to those he leads. A good leader will demand accountability of himself, and then he can be in a position to call others to accountable behaviour.

Leaders to admire

Those individual leaders whom we admire and respect are so regarded because they embody in many ways the qualities Jesus had in his life and leadership. History gives us many illustrations of leaders, both secular and religious, who had tragic impact on humanity.

Where Jesus was concerned with freedom they were concerned with control. Where Jesus was concerned with service they were concerned with status.

Where Jesus met the needs of others they were concerned only with their own needs.

Where Jesus was concerned with development of his followers they sought to manipulate their followers. Where Jesus was filled with compassion and justice they were filled with violence, harshness and injustice.

The message of Jesus was simple and straight forward; sometimes we complicate it and put our own slant on it to suit our purpose.

The following illustrates this.

THE LESSON[5]

Then Jesus took his disciples up to the mountain and gathering them around him, he taught them, saying "Blessed are the poor in spirit for theirs is the kingdom of heaven. Blessed are the meek. Blessed are they that mourn. Blessed are the merciful. Blessed are they that thirst for justice. Blessed are you when persecuted. Blessed are you when you suffer. Be glad and rejoice for your reward is great in heaven."

Then Simon Peter said "Do we have to write this down?"

And Andrew said "Are we supposed to know this?"

And James said "Will we have a test on this?"

And Phillip said "I don't have any paper!"

And Bartholomew said "Do we have to turn this in?"

And John said "The other disciples didn't have to learn this!"

And Matthew said "Can I go to the boys' room?"

And Judas said "What does this have to do with real life?"

Then one of the Pharisees who was present asked to see Jesus' lesson plan and inquired of Jesus: "Where are your anticipatory set and objectives in the cognitive domain?"

And Jesus wept!

A MODERN LORD'S PRAYER[6]

Our Father, who shall be termed party of the first part, whose place of business is in Heaven, Hallowed be thy name.

Thy Kingdom, pursuant to terms and conditions, come.

Thy will, duly uncontested, be done on earth, insofar as existing statutes permit, as it is in Heaven.

Give us this Thirty-first day of March, 2014, our daily bread.

5 thinkforyourself.ie/.../then-Jesus-took-his-disciples-up-the-mountain-and
6 www.churchwithin.org/August'2010.html

Forgive us our debts, notwithstanding claims, and legal costs, as we, who shall be termed party of the second part, forgive our debtors.

And lead us not into temptation, i.e. sin, corruption, greed, gluttony, etc., but deliver us from evil, the nature of which shall be determined by the court. For thine is the Kingdom and the Power and pending appeal, the Glory forever. Amen.

LEADERSHIP AS JESUS TAUGHT[7]

We lead more by what we say than by listening.

We lead more by doing than being.

We lead more by making things happen than by allowing them to happen.

We lead more by being in control than by surrender.

We lead more by comparing than by accepting.

We lead more from the head than from the heart.

We lead more by external change than internal change.

We lead according to how others react rather than by being rooted in who we are. ~ Author Unknown

JESUS AS CEO

Mary Ruth Swope,[8] author of eight management books says: "In my opinion, the most effective leader was Jesus.

He spearheaded the concept of servant leadership-Jesus knew who he was and showed that being a servant is the best way to behave in leadership."

Jesus taught that you did not have to be a hero to be a leader. He taught just the opposite; that to be a leader you must be

---

7 Leadership poems, www.bellaonline.com/articles/art38285.asp
8 https://www.facebook.com/pages/Jesus-CEO/149469388529840?ref.

a servant. He taught that there is no need to pull rank on each other. Jesus had twelve disciples whom he led and mentored and they, in turn, were sent out to further the work he was doing.

Jesus was willing to "walk the talk" and he demonstrated his commitment to this principle by the way he served others. Perhaps the most relevant example of what Jesus thought about heroic corporate leadership versus servant leadership is recorded in Matthew 20.

The mother of James and John came to Jesus and asked that her sons be permitted to sit at the right and left of Jesus in the Kingdom. Obviously, the mother of these two men had a very corporate view of the kingdom.

She wanted her sons to be at high points on the executive ladder, Executive Vice-Presidents of the Kingdom of God. Jesus did not agree with this management style. He pointed to the Gentiles as a bad example of those who "lord it over" people and wanted no part of this plan. Instead he pronounced a dictum he repeated on many occasions: "Whoever wants to be great among you must be your servant." Jesus modelled this style himself.

He said, "The Son of Man did not come to be served, but to serve, and to give his life as a ransom for many." Servant leadership may be a style of management to corporations but to Jesus it was an attitude of heart.

The next chapter looks at several inspirational stories on leadership.

Chapter Ten

Inspirational Leadership stories

As human beings, we continually tell ourselves stories -- of success or failure; of power or *victimhood*; stories that endure for an hour or a day or an entire lifetime. We have stories about our work, our families and relationships. Stories affect how others see us and how we see ourselves. Stories can transform and inspire life. The best leaders are good storytellers.

The best teachers and trainers and coaches are good storytellers. This chapter is a collection of inspirational stories on leadership.

The frogs who wanted to be king

Aesop[1] tells the story of the frogs who wanted a king. They annoyed Jupiter with their request until he finally tossed a log

---

1   Portraits of Pastoral Leadership: From Floating Logs to Preying Stork, www.directionjournal. org/8/2/portraits-of-pastoral-leadership

into the pond. For a while the frogs were happy with their new leader. Soon, however, they discovered that they could jump up and down on their leader and run all over him.

He offered no resistance nor gave any response.

He merely floated back and forth on the pond, a practice which finally exasperated the frogs who were really sincere about wanting "strong leadership". So back to Jupiter they went, complaining about their log leader and appealing for much stronger administrative oversight.

Jupiter was weary of the tiresome frogs so this time he gave them a stork that stood tall above the members of the group. He certainly had the appearance of a leader. The frogs were quite happy with the new situation.

Their leader stalked around the pond making impressive noises and attracting great attention. Their joy turned to sorrow, however, and then to panic when very soon the stork began eating his subjects.

HOW TO INSPIRE YOUR TEAM[2]

Be passionate

Be honest about your weaknesses

Care about people

Become a storyteller

Go beyond what is expected

Be responsible but not accountable for everything

The Janitor

I came across this great story on the net[3] and have given an abridged version here:

2   http://www.torontoismine.com/2012/11/top-tips-to-inspire-your-team/
3   www.homeofheroes.com/profiles/profiles_crawford_10lessons.html

William "Bill" Crawford certainly was an unimpressive figure, one you could easily overlook during a hectic day at the U.S. Air Force Academy.

Mr. Crawford was our squadron janitor. While the cadets busied themselves preparing for academic exams, athletic events, Saturday morning parades, leadership classes and so on Bill quietly moved about the squadron mopping and buffing floors, emptying trash cans, cleaning toilets or just tidying up the mess.

Sadly, and for many years, none of the cadets gave him much notice, rendering little more than a passing nod or throwing a curt, "G'morning!" in his direction as they hurried off to our daily duties. After all, cleaning toilets was his job, not theirs.

Maybe it was his physical appearance that made him disappear into the background. Bill didn't move very quickly and in fact, you could say he even shuffled a bit, as if he suffered from some sort of injury. His grey hair and wrinkled face made him appear ancient to the group of young cadets.

Face it, Bill was an old man working in a young person's world. What did he have to offer them on a personal level? Finally, maybe it was Mr. Crawford's personality that rendered him almost invisible to the young people around him. Bill was shy, almost painfully so.

He seldom spoke to a cadet unless they addressed him first and that didn't happen very often. Their janitor always buried himself in his work, moving about with stooped shoulders, a quiet gait and an averted gaze.

If he noticed the hustle and bustle of cadet life around him, it was hard to tell. That changed one fall Saturday afternoon in 1976. One of the cadets was reading a book about World War II and the tough Allied ground campaign in Italy, when he stumbled across an incredible story.

On Sept. 13, 1943, a Private William Crawford from Colorado, assigned to the 36th Infantry Division, had been involved in some bloody fighting on Hill 424 near Altavilla, Italy.

The words on the page leapt out "in the face of intense and overwhelming hostile fire ... with no regard for personal safety on his own initiative, Private Crawford single-handedly attacked fortified enemy positions."

It continued "for conspicuous gallantry and intrepidity at risk of life above and beyond the call of duty, the President of the United States ..." "Holy cow," said the cadet to his roommate, "you're not going to believe this, but I think our janitor is a Medal of Honour winner."

On Hill 424, Pvt. Crawford took out 3 enemy machine guns before darkness fell, halting the platoon's advance. Pvt. Crawford could not be found and was assumed dead. The request for his MOH was quickly approved.

MG Terry Allen presented the posthumous MOH to Bill Crawford's father, George, on 11 May 1944 in Camp (now Fort) Carson, near Pueblo. Nearly two months after that, it was learned that Pvt. Crawford was alive in a POW camp in Germany. During his captivity, a German guard clubbed him with his rifle. Bill overpowered him, took the rifle away and beat the guard unconscious.

A German doctor's testimony saved him from severe punishment, perhaps death.

To stay ahead of the advancing Russian army, the prisoners were marched 500 miles in 52 days in the middle of the German winter, subsisting on one potato a day.

An allied tank column liberated the camp in the spring of 1945 and Pvt. Crawford took his first hot shower in 18 months on VE Day.

Pvt. Crawford stayed in the army before retiring as a MSG and becoming a janitor.

We all knew Mr. Crawford was a WWII Army vet but that didn't keep my friend from looking at me as if I was some sort of alien being. Nonetheless, they couldn't wait to ask Bill about the story on Monday.

He stared at it for a few silent moments and then quietly uttered something like "Yep, that's me." "Why didn't you ever tell us about it?" He slowly replied after some thought, "That was one day in my life and it happened a long time ago."

However, after that brief exchange, things were never again the same around the squadron.

Word spread like wildfire among the cadets that we had a hero in our midst - Mr. Crawford, the janitor, had won the Medal! Cadets who had once passed by Bill with hardly a glance, now greeted him with a smile and a respectful, "Good morning, Mr. Crawford."

Those who before left a mess for the "janitor" to clean up started taking it upon themselves to put things in order. Most cadets routinely stopped to talk to Bill throughout the day and even began inviting him to our formal squadron functions.

He'd show up dressed in a conservative dark suit and quietly talk to those who approached him, the only sign of his heroics being a simple blue, star-spangled lapel pin.

Almost overnight, Bill went from being a simple fixture in the squadron to one of our teammates.

Mr. Crawford changed too but you had to look closely to notice the difference. After that fall day in 1976, he seemed to move with more purpose, his shoulders didn't seem to be as stooped, he met our greetings with a direct gaze and a stronger "good morning" in return.

Mr. Crawford continued to work at the Academy and eventually retired in his native Colorado one of four Medal of Honour winners living in a small town. [4]

A wise person once said, "It's not life that's important, but those you meet along the way that make the difference."[5]

1. Be Cautious of Labels. Labels you place on people may define your relationship to them and bind their potential.

2. Everyone Deserves Respect.

3. Courtesy Makes a Difference.

4. Take Time to Know Your People.

5. Anyone Can Be a Hero.

6. Leaders Should Be Humble.

7. Pursue Excellence. No matter what task life hands you, do it well. Mr. Crawford modelled that philosophy.

8. Life is a Leadership Laboratory. All too often we look to some school or class to teach us about leadership when, in fact, life is a leadership laboratory.

Those you meet every day will teach you enduring lessons if you just take time to stop look and listen.

Stories of Leadership and new perspectives[6]

The story is about a man by the name of Larry Walters, a 33-year-old man who decided he wanted to see his neighbourhood from a new perspective.

So he went down to the local army surplus store and bought

4   Col. James Moschgat, 12th Operations Group Commander Graduate United States Air Force Academy - class of 1977
5   ibid p.4
6   www.sermonillustrations.com/a-z/a/adventure.htm

forty-five used weather balloons. That afternoon he strapped himself into a lawn chair to which several of his friends tied the now helium-filled used weather balloons.

He took with him something to drink, a peanut-butter-and-jelly sandwich and a BB gun, figuring he could shoot the balloons one at a time when he was ready to land.

Walters, who assumed the balloons would lift him about 100 feet in the air, was caught off guard when the chair soared more than 11,000 feet into the sky--smack into the middle of the air traffic pattern at Los Angeles International Airport.

Because he was too frightened to shoot any of the balloons, he stayed airborne for more than two hours and forced the airport to shut down its runways for much of the afternoon. Soon after he was safely grounded and cited by the police, reporters asked him three questions:

"Were you scared?"

"Yes."

"Would you do it again?"

"No."

"Why did you do it?"

"Because you can't just sit there."

Monkey noise[7]

The story is told of a terrible traffic accident. Police officers were called to the scene and when they arrived they found a husband, wife and 2 children lying unconscious in the car.

They pulled them from the car and as they waited for the paramedics to arrive they noticed a monkey in the car also.

Seeing that the monkey was the only witness to the accident

7   www.sermoncentral.com/.../the-officers-in-the-church-gene-Gregory-ser

who was conscious, the officers decided to question him about the accident. Turning to the monkey they asked, "What was the dad doing at the time of the accident?" The monkey motioned, indicating that the dad had been drinking. The officers next asked what the mother had been doing at the time of the accident.

The monkey took his finger and shook it angrily at the unconscious man. The officers then asked what the children had been doing. The monkey this time indicated by hand gestures that the children had been fighting in the back seat.

The officers said, "Well, no wonder there was an accident with all of that going on in the car." As they turned to leave, almost as a parting thought they asked, "By the way, what were you doing at the time of the accident?" To which the monkey signed that he had been the one driving. It is important to remember that noise does not equal leadership.

The soldiers and the trench story[8]

The story goes that sometime, close to a battlefield over 200 years ago, a man in civilian clothes rode past a small group of exhausted battle-weary soldiers digging an obviously important defensive position. The section leader, making no effort to help, was shouting orders, threatening punishment if the work was not completed within the hour.

"Why are you are not helping?" asked the stranger on horseback. "I am in charge. The men do as I tell them," said the section leader, adding "Help them yourself if you feel strongly about it." To the section leader's surprise the stranger dismounted and helped the men until the job was finished. Before leaving the stranger congratulated the men for their work and approached the puzzled section leader.

"You should notify top command next time your rank prevents you from supporting your men - and I will provide a more permanent solution," said the stranger.

Up close, the section leader now recognized General Washington and also the lesson he'd just been taught.

(This story is allegedly based on truth.)

The shoes story⁹

You will perhaps have heard this very old story illustrating the difference between positive thinking and negative thinking: Many years ago two salesmen were sent by a British shoe manufacturer to Africa to investigate and report back on market potential.

The first salesman reported back, "There is no potential here - nobody wears shoes."The second salesman reported back, "There is massive potential here - nobody wears shoes."

This simple short story provides one of the best examples of how a single situation may be viewed in two quite different ways - negatively or positively.

We could explain this also in terms of seeing a situation's problems and disadvantages, instead of its opportunities and benefits. It is a good illustration of leadership.

Vision¹⁰

A man and a young teenage boy checked in to a hotel and were shown to their room. The two receptionists noted the quiet manner of the guests and the pale appearance of the boy.

Later the man and boy ate dinner in the hotel restaurant.

The staff again noticed that the two guests were very quiet

9   www.linkedin.com/.../Shoes-Story-positive-thinking-negative-102651.S....
10 www.businessballs.com › amusement/stress relief

and that the boy seemed disinterested in his food. After eating, the boy went to his room and the man went to reception and asked to see the manager.

The receptionist initially asked if there was a problem with the service or the room and offered to fix things but the man said that there was no problem of that sort and repeated his request.

The manager was called and duly appeared.

The man asked to speak privately and was taken into the manager's office.

The man explained that he was spending the night in the hotel with his fourteen-year-old son, who was seriously ill, probably terminally so.

The boy was very soon to undergo therapy which would cause him to lose his hair. They had come to the hotel to have a break together and also because the boy planned to shave his head that night rather than feel that the illness was beating him. The father said that he would be shaving his own head too, in support of his son. He asked that staff be respectful when the two of them came to breakfast with their shaved heads.

The manager assured the father that he would inform all staff and that they would behave appropriately.

The following morning the father and son entered the restaurant for breakfast. There they saw the four male restaurant staff attending to their duties, perfectly normally, all with shaved heads.

The gardener's badge story[11]

A landscape gardener ran a business that had been in the family for two or three generations.

11 wholechildcreativecurriculum.blogspot.com/.../more-business-stories.htm...

The staff was happy and customers loved to visit the store or to have the staff work on their gardens or make deliveries - anything from bedding plants to ride-on mowers.

For as long as anyone could remember, the current owner and previous generations of owners were extremely positive happy people. Most folk assumed it was because they ran a successful business. In fact it was the other way around...

A tradition in the business was that the owner always wore a big lapel badge saying Business Is Great!

The business was indeed generally great although it went through tough times like any other. What never changed however was the owner's attitude and the badge saying Business Is Great! Everyone who saw the badge for the first time invariably asked, "What's so great about business?" Sometimes people would also comment that their own business was miserable or even that they personally were miserable or stressed.

The Badge always tended to start a conversation, which typically involved the owner talking about lots of positive aspects of business and work, for example:

> the pleasure of meeting and talking with different people every day

> the reward that comes from helping staff take on new challenges and experiences

> the fun and laughter in a relaxed and healthy work environment

> the fascination in the work itself and in the other people's work and businesses

> the great feeling when you finish a job and do it to the best of your capabilities

> the new things you learn every day - even without looking to do so

And so the list went on. And no matter how miserable a person was, they'd usually end up feeling a lot happier after just a couple of minutes listening to all this infectious enthusiasm and positivity.

It is impossible to quantify or measure attitude like this but to one extent or another it's probably a self-fulfilling prophecy: "The badge came first. The great business followed."

The trench-digger – Self belief[12]

This is adapted from (apparently) a true story.

An elderly couple retired to the countryside - to a small isolated cottage overlooking some rugged and rocky land.

One early morning the woman saw from her window a young man dressed in working clothes walking on the heath, about a hundred yards away. He was carrying a spade and a small case and he disappeared from view behind a copse of trees. The woman thought no more about it but around the same time the next day she saw the man again, carrying his spade and a small case and again he disappeared behind the copse of trees.

The woman mentioned this to her husband, who said he was probably a farmer or gamekeeper setting traps or performing some other country practice that would be perfectly normal and so not to worry. However after several more sightings of the young man with the spade over the next two weeks the woman persuaded her husband to take a stroll , early, before the man tended to arrive, to the copse of trees to investigate what he was doing. There they found a surprisingly long and deep trench, rough and uneven at one end, becoming much neater and tidier towards the other end.

12 Stories, analogies and fables for business, training and public... www.businessballs.com › amusement/stress relief

"How strange," the old lady said, "Why dig a trench here and in such difficult rocky ground?" and her husband agreed.

Just then the young man appeared - earlier than his usual time.

"You're early," said the old woman, making light of their obvious curiosity. "We wondered what you were doing - and we also wondered what was in the case."

"I'm digging a trench," said the man, who continued, realising a bigger explanation was appropriate.

"I'm actually learning how to dig a good trench because the job I'm being interviewed for later today says that experience is essential - so I'm getting the experience. And the case - it's got my lunch in it." He got the job.

Mirror-Mirror[13]

A school head was alerted by the caretaker to a persistent problem in the girl's toilets. Some of the girls were leaving lipstick kisses on the mirrors. The caretaker had left notices on the toilet walls asking for the practice to cease but to no avail; every evening the caretaker would wipe away the kisses and the next day lots more kisses would be planted on the mirror. It had become a bit of a game.

The head teacher usually took a creative approach to problem solving and so the next day she asked a few girl representatives from each class to meet with her in the lavatory. Thank you for coming," said the head, "You will see there are several lipstick kisses in the mirrors in this wash-room."Some of the girls grinned at each other. "As you will understand, modern lipstick is cleverly designed to stay on the lips and so the lipstick is not easy at all to clean from the mirrors.

13 ibid p. 25.

We have therefore had to develop a special cleaning regime and my hope is that when you see the effort involved you will help spread the word that we'd all be better off if those responsible for the kisses use tissue paper instead of the mirrors in future."

At this point the caretaker stepped forward with a sponge squeegee, which he took into one of the toilet cubicles, dipped into the toilet bowl and then used to clean one of the lipstick-covered mirrors. The caretaker smiled. The girls departed. And there were no more lipstick kisses on the mirrors. There are teachers and then there are educators!

Shot at dawn[14]

By December 1916 more than 17,000 British troops were officially diagnosed as suffering from nervous or mental disability, (we'd say shell-shock or post-traumatic stress disorder these days) despite which the British military authorities continued to charge and convict sufferers with 'cowardice' and 'desertion', and to sentence to death by firing squad many of those found 'guilty'.

On 16 August 2006 the British government announced that it would pardon 308 British soldiers who were shot by firing squad for 'cowardice' and 'desertion' during the First World War of 1914-18. The decision was ratified by Parliament on 7 November 2006 and represented a remarkable U-Turn by this and previous governments who had always firmly refuted any evidence and justification for pardoning the victims.[15] This reversal followed and was largely due to decades of persistent lobbying and campaigning by organisations and individuals, many being families and descendants of the victims.

14 ibid p.26
15 www.curiousnerve.com/2013/02/16/a-simple-story-about-change

It is not easy to imagine their suffering, especially of the widows and parents long since gone, for whom this decision came a lifetime too late.

The story emphasises two things: first, that people in authority have a responsibility to behave with integrity. Second, that where people in authority fail to act with integrity, the persistence and determination of ordinary people will eventually force them to do so.

We've always done it this way[16]

One of the most common reactions to change in leadership is for people to say 'we have always done it this way, so why change?' A little girl was watching her mother prepare a fish for dinner. Her mother cut the head and tail off the fish and then placed it into a baking pan.

The little girl asked her mother why she cut the head and tail off the fish. Her mother thought for a while and then said, "I've always done it that way - that's how my grandmother did it." Not satisfied with the answer, the little girl went to visit her grandma to find out why she cut the head and tail off the fish before baking it. Grandma thought for a while and replied, "I don't know. My mother always did it that way."

So the little girl and the grandma went to visit great grandma to find ask if she knew the answer. Great grandma thought for a while and said, "Because my baking pan was too small to fit in the whole fish".

The owl and the field-mouse[17]

A little field-mouse was lost in a dense wood unable to find his way out. He came upon a wise old owl sitting in a tree.

16 https://www.facebook.com/problemschalhut?ref=stream&filter
17 yourcoachingsolution.com/leadership-is-a-choice

"Please help me, wise old owl, how can I get out of this wood?" said the field-mouse.

"Easy," said the owl, "Grow wings and fly out, as I do."

"But how can I grow wings?" asked the mouse.

The owl looked at him haughtily, sniffed disdainfully and said, "Don't bother me with the details, I only decide the policy." Good leadership is not just about theory. It also calls for practical solutions.

Charles Plumb parachutes story[18]

Charles Plumb was a navy jet pilot. On his seventy-sixth combat mission, he was shot down and parachuted into enemy territory. He was captured and spent six years in prison. One day, a man approached Plumb and his wife in a restaurant and said, "Are you Plumb the navy pilot?"

"Yes, how did you know?" asked Plumb.

"I packed your parachute," the man replied.

Plumb was amazed and grateful: "If the chute you packed hadn't worked I wouldn't be here today..." Plumb refers to this in his lectures: his realisation that the anonymous sailors who packed the parachutes held the pilots' lives in their hands and yet the pilots never gave these sailors a second thought; never even said hello, let alone said thanks. Now Plumb asks his audiences, "Who packs your parachutes?"

Managers and secretaries[19]

A big corporation hired several cannibals. "You are all part of our team now," said the Human Resource manager during the welcome briefing. "You get all the usual benefits and you can go

18 www.torah.org/learning/dvartorah/5773/vayechi.html
19 www.citehr.com › Human Resource Section › Motivation & Improvement

to the cafeteria for something to eat but please don't eat any of the other employees." The cannibals promised they would not.

A few weeks later the cannibal's boss remarked, "You're all working very hard and I'm satisfied with you. However, one of our secretaries has disappeared. Do any of you know what happened to her?" The cannibals all shook their heads, "No," they said.

After the boss left, the leader of the cannibals said to the others angrily, "Right, which one of you idiots ate the secretary?" A hand rose hesitantly in admission. "You fool!" said the leader. "For weeks we've been eating managers and no one noticed anything but you had to go and eat someone important!"

Organisational development and Leadership[20]

Start with a cage containing five monkeys.

Inside the cage, hang a banana on a string and place a set of stairs under it. Before long, a monkey will go to the stairs and start to climb towards the banana. As soon as he touches the stairs, spray all of the monkeys with cold water. After a while, another monkey makes an attempt with the same result - all the monkeys are sprayed with cold water.

Pretty soon, when another monkey tries to climb the stairs, the other monkeys will try to prevent it. Now, turn off the cold water. Remove one monkey from the cage and replace it with a new one. The new monkey sees the banana and wants to climb the stairs. To his surprise and horror, all of the other monkeys attack him. After another attempt and attack, he knows that if he tries to climb the stairs, he will be assaulted.

Next, remove another of the original five monkeys and replace it with a new one. The newcomer goes to the stairs and is attacked.

20 creativethinking.net/DA13, tales of five monkeys.htm

The previous newcomer takes part in the punishment with enthusiasm. Again, replace a third original monkey with a new one. The new one makes it to the stairs and is attacked as well.

Two of the four monkeys that beat him have no idea why they were not permitted to climb the stairs or why they are participating in the beating of the newest monkey.

After replacing the fourth and fifth original monkeys, all the monkeys that have been sprayed with cold water have been replaced. Nevertheless, no monkey ever again approaches the stairs. Why not? Because as far as they know that's the way it's always been around here.

And that's how company policy begins.

Chapter Eleven

101 Famous quotes on Leadership

Parker Palmer says: 'A leader is someone with the power to project either shadow or light onto some part of the world and onto the lives of people who dwell there.'[1]

There are times in life when you are called upon to say a few inspiring words to your team, your staff and your fellow workers.

A good quote often sums up what you want to say. In this chapter I have gathered together a list of quotes from famous people. This list is by no means exhaustive but it will give you a start. It is better to lead from behind and to put others in front, especially when you celebrate victory when nice things occur.

You take the front line when there is danger.

Then people will appreciate your leadership. [2]

Quotes on Leadership[3]

1. Nelson Mandela

If you think you can do a thing or think you can't do a thing, you're right.

2. Henry Ford

A genuine leader is not a searcher for consensus but a moulder of consensus.

3. Martin Luther King, Jr.

A leader is best when people barely know he exists, when his work is done, his aim fulfilled, they will say: we did it ourselves.

4. Lao Tzu

Leadership is solving problems. The day soldiers stop bringing you their problems is the day you have stopped leading them. They have either lost confidence that you can help or concluded you do not care. Either case is a failure of leadership.

5. Colin Powell

Effective leadership is not about making speeches or being liked; leadership is defined by results not attributes.

6. Peter Drucker

If your actions inspire others to dream more, learn more, do more and become more, you are a leader.

7. John Quincy Adams

People ask the difference between a leader and a boss. he leader leads and the boss drives. A man who wants to lead the orchestra must turn his back on the crowd.

---

2   http://www.brainyquote.com/quotes/topics/topic_leadership.html
3   Quotes 1 - 9 ibid; 11- 24 ibid and 26 – 64 ibid

8. Max Lucado

Leadership is the art of getting someone else to do something you want done because he wants to do it.

9. Dwight D. Eisenhower

He who has never learned to obey cannot be a good commander.

10. Aristotle[4]

No man will make a great leader who wants to do it all himself or to get all the credit for doing it.

11. Andrew Carnegie

A true leader has the confidence to stand alone, the courage to make tough decisions and the compassion to listen to the needs of others.

He does not set out to be a leader but becomes one by the equality of his actions and the integrity of his intent.

12. Douglas MacArthur

No man is good enough to govern another man without that other's consent.

13. Abraham Lincoln

Leadership is practiced not so much in words as in attitude and actions.

14. Harold Geneen

We live in a society obsessed with public opinion. But leadership has never been about popularity.

15. Marco Rubio

To have long term success as a coach or in any position of leadership, you have to be obsessed in some way.

16. Pat Riley

Leadership is the capacity to translate vision into reality.

17. Warren Bennis

Leaders think and talk about the solutions. Followers think and talk about the problems.

18. Brian Tracy

Never tell people how to do things. Tell them what to do and they will surprise you with their ingenuity.

19. General George Patton

You manage things; you lead people.

20. Admiral Grace Murray Hopper

Leadership and learning are indispensable to each other.

21. John F. Kennedy

Outstanding leaders go out of their way to boost the self-esteem of their personnel.

If people believe in themselves, it's amazing what they can accomplish.

22. Sam Walton

Leadership is lifting a person's vision to high sights, the raising of a person's performance to a higher standard, the building of a personality beyond its normal limitations.

23. Peter Drucker

The first responsibility of a leader is to define reality. The last is to say thank you. In between, the leader is a servant.

24. Max DePree

Where there is no vision, the people perish.

25. Proverbs 29:18[5]

I must follow the people. Am I not their leader?

26. Benjamin Disraeli

Lead me, follow me or get out of my way.

27. General George Patton

Before you are a leader, success is all about growing yourself.

When you become a leader, success is all about growing others.

28. Jack Welch

A leader is a dealer in hope.

29. Napoleon Bonaparte

A leader is one who knows the way, goes the way and shows the way.

30. John Maxwell

My own definition of leadership is this: The capacity and the will to rally men and women to a common purpose and the character which inspires confidence.

31. General Montgomery

Leadership is lifting a person's vision to high sights, the raising of a person's performance to a higher standard, the building of a personality beyond its normal limitations.

32. Peter Drucker

Never doubt that a small group of thoughtful, concerned citizens can change world. Indeed it is the only thing that ever has.

5   http://www.forbes.com/sites/kevinkruse/2012/10/16/quotes-on-leadership

33. Margaret Mead

The most dangerous leadership myth is that leaders are born-that there is a genetic factor to leadership. That's nonsense; in fact, the opposite is true. Leaders are made rather than born.

34. Warren Bennis

To command is to serve, nothing more and nothing less.

35. Andre Malraux

He who has never learned to obey cannot be a good commander.

36. Aristotle

I start with the premise that the function of leadership is to produce more leaders, not more followers

37. Ralph Nader

Anyone can hold the helm when the sea is calm.

38. Publilius Syrus

The art of leadership is saying no, not saying yes.

It is very easy to say yes.

39. Tony Blair

A good general not only sees the way to victory; he also knows when victory is impossible

40. Polybius

A great leader's courage to fulfil his vision comes from passion, not position.

41. John Maxwell

A leader takes people where they want to go.

A great leader takes people where they don't necessarily want to go, but ought to be.

42. Rosalynn Carter

A true leader has the confidence to stand alone, the courage to make tough decisions and the compassion to listen to the needs of others.

He does not set out to be a leader, but becomes one by the equality of his actions and the integrity of his intent.

43. Douglas MacArthur

The leader has to be practical and a realist yet must talk the language of the visionary and the idealist

44. Eric Hoffer

Leaders think and talk about the solutions.

Followers think and talk about the problems

45. Brian Tracy

As we look ahead into the next century, leaders will be those who empower others.

46. Bill Gates

All of the great leaders have had one characteristic in common: it was the willingness to confront unequivocally the major anxiety of their people in their time.

This, and not much else, is the essence of leadership.

47. John Kenneth Galbraith

Do what you feel in your heart to be right–for you'll be criticized anyway

48. Eleanor Roosevelt

Effective leadership is putting first things first. Effective management is discipline, carrying it out.

49. Stephen Covey

He who has great power should use it lightly.

50. Seneca

I cannot give you the formula for success, but I can give you the formula for failure, which is:

Try to please everybody.

51. Herbert Swope

It is absurd that a man should rule others, who cannot rule himself.

52. Latin Proverb

Leaders aren't born, they are made. And they are made just like anything else, through hard work.

And that's the price we'll have to pay to achieve that goal, or any goal.

53. Vince Lombardi

Leadership cannot just go along to get along. Leadership must meet the moral challenge of the day.

54. Jesse Jackson

Leadership is solving problems.

The day soldiers stop bringing you their problems is the day you have stopped leading them.

55. Stephen Covey

No man is good enough to govern another man without that other's consent.

56. Abraham Lincoln

What you do has far greater impact than what you say.

57. Stephen Covey

Not the cry, but the flight of a wild duck, leads the flock to fly and follow.

58. Walter Lippmann

The growth and development of people is the highest calling of leadership.

59. Harvey Firestone

To do great things is difficult; but to command great things is more difficult.

60. Friedrich Nietzsche

True leadership lies in guiding others to success. In ensuring that everyone is performing at their best, doing the work they are pledged to do and doing it well.

61. Bill Owens

A good leader is a person who takes a little more than his share of the blame and a little less than his share of the credit.

62. John Maxwell

There are three essentials to leadership: humility, clarity and courage.

63. Fuchan Yuan

The supreme quality of leadership is integrity. Without it there is no real success

64. Dwight D. Eisenhower

Don't underestimate the power of a vision. McDonald's founder, Ray Kroc, pictured his empire long before it existed and he saw how to get there.

My personal favourite quotes[6]

He invented the company motto — 'Quality, service, cleanliness and value' — and kept repeating it to employees for the rest of his life.

Kenneth Labich (65) [7]

I've missed more than 9000 shots in my career. I've lost almost 300 games. 26 times. I've been trusted to take the game winning shot and missed. I've failed over and over and over again in my life. And that is why I succeed.

Michael Jordan (66)

Life is 10% what happens to me and 90% of how I react to it.

Charles Swindoll (67)

Eighty percent of success is showing up.

Woody Allen (68)

Your time is limited, so don't waste it living someone else's life.

Steve Jobs (69)

I am not a product of my circumstances. I am a product of my decisions.

Stephen Covey (70)

Whatever you can do, or dream you can, begin it. Boldness has genius, power and magic in it.

6   Quote 66-88 ibid and 90-95 ibid
7   http://www.forbes.com/sites/kevinkruse/2012/10/16/quotes-on-leadership

Johann Wolfgang von Goethe (71)

There is only one way to avoid criticism: Do nothing, say nothing and be nothing.

Aristotle (72)

The only person you are destined to become is the person you decide to be.

Ralph Waldo Emerson (73)

Go confidently in the direction of your dreams. Live the life you have imagined.

Henry David Thoreau (74)

Believe you can and you're halfway there.

Theodore Roosevelt (75)

You can't fall if you don't climb. But there's no joy in living your whole life on the ground.

Unknown (76)

Too many of us are not living our dreams because we are living our fears

Les Brown (77)

In order to succeed, your desire for success should be greater than your fear of failure.

Bill Cosby (78)

The person who says it cannot be done should not interrupt the person who is doing it.

Chinese Proverb (79)

There are no traffic jams along the extra mile.

Roger Staubach (80)

You become what you believe.

Oprah Winfrey (81)

I have learned over the years that when one's mind is made up, this diminishes fear.

Rosa Parks (82)

It does not matter how slowly you go as long as you do not stop.

Confucius (83)

The question isn't who is going to let me; it's who is going to stop me.

Ayn Rand (84)

When everything seems to be going against you, re-member that the airplane takes off against the wind, not with it.

Henry Ford (85)

Change your thoughts and you change your world.

Norman Vincent Peale (86)

If you can dream it, you can achieve it.

Zig Ziglar (87)

Leadership happens at every level of the organisation and no one can shirk from this responsibility.

Jerry Junkins (88)

The real leader has no need to lead—he is content to point the way.

Henry Miller (89)[8]

A leader's dynamic does not come from special powers. It comes from a strong belief in a purpose and a willingness to express that conviction.

Kouzes & Posner (90)

Inspired leaders move a business beyond problems into opportunities.

Dr. Abraham Zaleznik (91)

Truly great leaders spend as much time collecting and acting upon feedback as they do providing it

Alexander Lucia (92)

The best leader is the one who has sense enough to pick good people to do what he/she wants done, and self-restraint enough to keep from meddling with them while they do it.

Theodore Roosevelt (93)

If leaders are careless about basic things - telling the truth, respecting moral codes, proper professional conduct - who can believe them on other issues?

James L Hayes (94)

The key to successful leadership today is influence, not authority.

Ken Blanchard (95)

If you really want people to respond to your leadership, you have to have a personal relationship with them.

They need to know you're dependable and that you'll be there if they have a problem. That's personal power to me.

Noreen Heffner (96) [9]

Only one man in a thousand is a leader of men -- the other 999 follow women.

Groucho Marx (97) [10]

Some believe there is nothing one man or one woman can do against the enormous array of the world's ills ; against misery, against ignorance, or injustice and violence. Yet many of the world's great movements, of thought and action, have flowed from the work of a single man.

A young monk began the Protestant reformation, a young general extended an empire from Macedonia to the borders of the earth and a young woman reclaimed the territory of France.

It was a young Italian explorer who discovered the New World and 32 year old Thomas Jefferson who proclaimed that all men are created equal. 'Give me a place to stand,' said Archimedes, 'and I will move the world.' These men moved the world, and so can we all.

Robert F. Kennedy (98) [11]

9 http://quotations.about.com/od/funnymovieandtvquotes/a/grouchomarx5.htm
10 https://www.leadershipnow.com/visionquotes
11 blog.gaiam.com/quotes/authors/Robert-kenned

If you want to build a ship, don't herd people together to collect wood and don't assign them tasks and work, but rather teach them to long for the endless immensity of the sea.

Antoine de Saint-Exupery (99) [12]

A sense of humour is part of the art of leadership, of getting along with people, of getting things done.

Dwight D. Eisenhower (100) [13]

Leadership is about change... The best way to get people to venture into unknown terrain is to make it desirable by taking them there in their imaginations

Noel Tichy (101) [14]

12 quotations.about.com/od/.../a/AntoinedeSaint1.
13 https://www.goodreads.com/.../36270-a-sense-of-humor-is-part-of-the-ar
14 ilmlevel2.wikispaces.com/file/view/Leading+the+Team.

Chapter Twelve

General leadership principles

"You do not lead by hitting people over the head — that's assault, not leadership." – Dwight Eisenhower[1]

So far we have looked at leadership in a broad spectrum.

There are some general principles worth knowing and understanding in the leadership field.

A principle may be defined as an accepted or professed rule of action or conduct: a moral rule that helps you know what is right or wrong; an idea that forms the basis of something and a law or fact that explains how something works.[2]

You will find the Pareto principle and the principle of the lid explained here.

1   www.forbes.com/.../20-leadership-quotes-to-make-you-laugh
2   dictionary.reference.com/browse/in+principle > ⊠www.gassner.co.il/pareto

Pareto's Principle - The 80-20 Rule in Leadership[3]

In 1906, Italian economist Vilfredo Pareto created a mathematical formula to describe the unequal distribution of wealth in his country, observing that twenty percent of the people owned eighty percent of the wealth.

In the late 1940s, Dr. Joseph M. Juran inaccurately attributed the 80/20 Rule to Pareto, calling it Pareto's Principle. While it may be misnamed, Pareto's Principle or Pareto's Law as it is sometimes called can be a very effective tool to help you manage and lead effectively.[4]

What It Means

The 80/20 Rule means that in anything a few (20 percent) are vital and many (80 percent) are trivial. In Pareto's case it meant 20 percent of the people owned 80 percent of the wealth.

Project Managers and effective leaders know that 20 percent of the work (the first 10 percent and the last 10 percent) consume 80 percent of your time and resources. You can apply the 80/20 Rule to almost anything, from the science of management to the physical world.

You know 20 percent of your stock takes up 80 percent of your warehouse space and that 80 percent of your stock comes from 20 percent of your suppliers.

Also 80 percent of your sales will come from 20 percent of your sales staff. 20 percent of your staff will cause 80 percent of your problems, but another 20 percent of your staff will provide 80 percent of your production. It works both ways.

---

3 www.mindtools.com › Decision Making skills
4 www.forbes.com/.../20-leadership-quotes-to-make-you-laugh

How It Can Help You

The value of the Pareto Principle in leadership and management is that it reminds you to focus on the 20 percent that matters. Of the things you do during your day, only 20 percent really matter. Those 20 percent produce 80 percent of your results. Identify and focus on those things.

There is a management theory floating around in recent times that proposes to interpret Pareto's Principle in such a way as to produce what is called Superstar Management. The theory's supporters claim that since 20 percent of your people produce 80 percent of your results you should focus your limited time on managing only that 20 percent, the superstars.

This theory I believe is flawed because it overlooks the fact that 80 percent of your time should be spent doing what is really important. Helping the good become better is a better use of your time than helping the great become superstars. The Pareto Principle should be applied wisely.

"The very essence of leadership is that you have to have vision. You can't blow an uncertain trumpet."
Theodore M. Hesburgh[5].

Principle of the Lid[6]

John Maxwell introduced us to the leadership principle "The Law of the Lid" in his bestselling book, The 21 Irrefutable Laws of Leadership.. The Law of the Lid says this:

Leadership ability is the lid that determines a person's level of effectiveness.

5   http://www.transformingleader.org/lids-levels-and-leadership
6   www.christianpost.com › church & ministry, July 2010

This law states the lower an individual's ability to lead, the lower the lid on his potential; the higher the individual's ability to lead, the higher the lid on his potential.

To give you an example, if your leadership rates an 8, then your effectiveness can never be greater than a 7.

If your leadership is only a 4, then your effectiveness will be no higher than a 3. Your leadership ability – for better or for worse – always determines your effectiveness and the potential impact of your organization.[7]

The principle of the leadership lid is simple. An organisation can move no higher than the leadership qualities of the leader. Like any so-called principle, the leadership lid certainly has exceptions.

It is not an ironclad rule.

This principle suggests for instance, if the leader has character deficiencies, the organisation will suffer. Or if he or she has a work ethic problem, the organisation does not reach its potential.

Am I the Right Leader for My Organisation?

This question is the toughest for most leaders.[8]

We often assume that, if we have been given or assigned a leadership position, then we must be qualified for it. But the reality, of course, is that many leaders are ill-suited for their current position of leadership.

Regardless of the circumstances that brought them to the position, a number of leaders soon discover their deficiencies for the task outweigh their strengths.

---

7   The Principle of the Leadership Lid - ThomRainer.com
8   Based on the principles from > http://hbr.org/1998/03/the-set-up-to-fail-syndrome/ar/1, March 1998

Can I Make the Necessary Adjustments?[9]

In some situations, the leader can make the necessary adjustments. It may be something as basic as re-educating him/herself.

Or it could be that the organisational alignment is not optimal. Perhaps the leader is not a detailed person and he needs someone to compensate for that deficiency.

Selecting the right person is central to this.

Over my lifetime I have seen organisations select like minded people on leadership teams and this is disastrous. Everyone thinking the same way means no one is thinking.

Do You Have Sufficient Self-awareness?[10]

Good leaders though, find people who will shoot straight with them, who will let them know where they may be succeeding or failing as a leader.

Admittedly, such honest and straightforward friends are hard to find. And even if a leader finds such a person, the leader must have the willingness and courage to listen and respond to the tough facts.

The Lid and the Bus

In Jim Collins' book 'Good to Great'[11] he uses the metaphor of the bus. All great organisations make certain they get the right people on the bus. In other words, they bring the right people into the organisation. He then says we must get the right people into the right seats on the bus.

We can have great people in our organisation who prove

9   ibid 2
10 Principle of leadership lid, www.christianpost.com › church & ministry
11 www.forbes.com/.../20-leadership-quotes-to-make-you-laugh

ineffective because they are not in the right roles or as Collins puts it, the right seats on the bus. One of the great dangers of any organisation is having a leader who is in the wrong seat on the bus.

My brother, says organisations often promote people from a level of competence to incompetence. One might be a great teacher in a classroom but a poor head teacher. That leader, with whatever deficiencies he or she brings, is like a lid on the organisation. The organisation is limited because of the limitations of the leader.

As Franklin D. Roosevelt once said:"It is a terrible thing to look over your shoulder when you are trying to lead — and find no one there."[12]

Leadership growth is not static, we are always learning and adapting to the changing scenarios around us daily. Andy Pearson experienced a conversion of attitude late in life. His story follows: [13]

Andy Pearson-the man of nails

Andy Pearson founding chairman and former CEO of Tricon Global Restaurants Inc. (KFC, Pizza Hut, and Taco Bell) has recently undergone a huge change in leadership style.

The new Andy Pearson, a man who is now in his mid-70s, has transformed himself into a new kind of leader who majors on inspirational motivation.

Having carved himself a decades-long reputation of ruthless, hard-nosed, numbers-obsessed success in corporate America with companies such as Pepsi Cola and McKinsey; he now feels that he has arrived at a personal point of change that he feels has great significance for all in leadership.

12 www.evancarmichael.com/Management/.../Leadership-Styles--3-Key-Lessons
13 thoughts.forbes.com/.../executives-Theodore-Roosevelt-the-best- executives

Through working with colleagues at Tricom, Pearson experienced a conversion as he realised the importance of the human heart in driving a company's success - one person at a time - and how this kind of success can't be imposed from the top but must be ignited and nurtured through attention, awareness, recognition, reward and true inspirational motivation.

Pearson realised that the need for recognition is a fundamental human drive and key to inspirational motivation in change management situations. He changed his direction and style almost overnight.

Pearson says:"Great leaders find a balance between getting results and how they get them." He now believes that it's less important to issue orders than it is to seek answers and ideas from below. He sees his job is to listen to the people who work for him and to serve them. He still believes in firing those who don't perform!

Andy Pearson's experience shows that people benefit from a change in management- leadership style that addresses their emotional side and gives them respect and approval. People need to be included in the process before they feel ownership of it. Leadership is a process that doesn't happen in a day but over a life time as you continue to learn.

The story of Andy Pearson illustrates this. How then do we grow as leaders? Theodore Roosevelt: states "The best executive is the one who has sense enough to pick good men to do what he wants done, and self-restraint to keep from meddling with them while they do it." [14]

How can I grow as a leader?

Leadership develops daily, not in a day. The secret to success is found in our daily agenda.

14 Sean Ruth, Leadership and liberation ,2006

Our ability to lead is really a collection of skills, nearly all of which can be learned or improved.

Over the past 30 years running leadership workshops I have seen people develop skills and change their perspectives on themselves and life. Leadership training has various facets.

Respect for each person you train and for each person on the team or work force. Each person has an experience of life that colours how he or she sees things. Good leadership takes into account the various experiences of others and as Sean Ruth put it 'Listens into action and change. '[15]

Each person has emotional strength that differs from our own. We can't impose or force our own strength onto them. People skills, personal discipline, vision and timing are also central to leadership development.

Leadership growth happens in phases.

We start with I don't know what I don't know. Every one of us can lead but the problem is some of us think we don't have the ability. We assume that leadership is something imposed whereas it's something we take up and this is a choice we make.

Helping people discover what they don't know assists in the discovery of what they know. Sometimes a person realizes no one is following me so I need to learn how to lead.

Benjamin Disraeli, English Prime Minister, once said: 'to be conscious of the fact you are ignorant of the facts is a great step to knowledge'.[16]

Successful leaders are learners and learning is an ongoing process. When you recognize your lack of skills, the daily discipline of personal growth begins.

15 en.wikiquote.org/wiki/Benjamin Disraeli Letter to his father from Malta (25 August 1830), cited in Lord Beaconsfield's Letters
16 en.wikiquote.org/wiki/Benjamin Disraeli

Then exciting things start to happen. I have spent my life learning skills from different leaders I have met. To lead tomorrow, learn today. I have learnt that leadership is developed daily and is not static.

No matter where you are starting from you can get better. Everyone has the potential but it requires perseverance.

Psychology of leadership: What is it?

If leadership centres on the process of influence, then in order to understand it, we need to focus on the mental states that lead people to listen to leaders and to take on their vision. Leadership is not just a psychological phenomenon that can be explained by psychology alone.

Psychologists must pay attention to the social context and the nature of society. [17]

Good psychology will tell us what to look for in our society. In the case of leadership there are a range of contextual factors that impacts on a leader's ability to influence others. These include:

1. The culture of the group that is being led and the broader society, in which the group finds itself.

2. The nature of the institutions within which leadership takes place and

3. The gender of the leaders themselves.[18]

In any complex modern social group such as an army, a church or large organisation, we find three types of leaders.

The first is the leader who maintains authority mainly by virtue of established social prestige attached to the position.

17 Israel & Tajfel , 1972, , quoted in S, Alexander Haslam, Stephen D. Reicher and Michael J, Platow,p. xx.
18 ibid p.xx

Secondly there is the leader who maintains authority by virtue of a personal capacity to impress and dominate followers and thirdly there is the leader who maintains authority by virtue of a capacity to express and persuade followers.

The first is the Institutional type, the second the Dominant type and the third the Persuasive type.

Institutional Leader[19]

Such a leader maintains authority and builds up a thoroughly coherent group. The danger with this group is that it inevitably tends to become rather narrowly self-contained and non-adaptable. To exalt the symbol is the only way in which the leader whose power is in his/her post rather than in him/her can consolidate authority. [20]

If for instance a school has a principal whose leadership style is institutional he or she will be fussy about school uniform, formal discipline and a rigidity and love of the past.

There are many more leaders of this type than of any other. This type of leader will remain aloof from all beneath him/her.

Dominant Leader[21]

Let us say we have a dominant leader in an army group, who impresses, commands, shapes and sways his men/women.

This leader presents a number of extremely interesting psychological problems. The dominant leader draws power directly from the strength in him/her of the social instinct of assertiveness. The weakness in this type is that outside the particular army group this leader carries no sway.

---

19 www.bartlett.psychol.cam.ac.uk/TheSocialPsychOfLeader
20 www.bartlett.psychol.cam.ac.uk/TheSocialPsychOfLeader
21 www.forbes.com/sites/.../5-dominant-traits-of-successful-leader

Persuasive Leader[22]

The persuasive type of leader is, in many respects, psychologically the most interesting of all. He/she is, as a rule, very much the most complex and subtle character. This type of leader has always played an important part in social life but tends to come more and more to the front as society develops. [23]

This is the political type of leadership, the civil type, the administrative type. It is particularly in place in a settled community, within which there are a number of groups in fairly close contact and friendly relationship and a good deal of negotiation has to be carried on between them.

What counts as a leadership quality depends on the context in which leadership is needed. A politician's intelligence and judgements will be different to that of a soldier in the army.

Different contexts call for different forms of same the same quality. We cannot look at leadership in isolation of groups. This is wonderfully illustrated by Bertolt Fragen. [24]

Who built Thebes of the seven gates? In the books you will read the names of kings. Did the kings haul up the lumps of rock? The young Alexander conquered India.

Was he alone?

Caesar defeated the Gauls.

Did he even have a cook with him?

These rhetorical questions invite us to change our view of leadership as an activity that is exclusive rather than inclusive, personal rather than social and individual rather than collective.[25]

22 www.bartlett.psychol.cam.ac.uk/TheSocialPsychOfLeader
23 www.bartlett.psychol.cam.ac.uk/TheSocialPsychOfLeader
24 Brecht (1935/1976) poem 'Fragen eines lesenden Albeiters (Questions from a worker who reads)
25 cited in: S. Alexander Haslam, Stephen D. Reicher, Michael J. Platow - Psychology, 2013

Listening to the news bulletins each day, reading through the national news papers one is tempted to ask –is there any morality in leadership today? What about moral leadership?

This is explored in the next chapter.

Chapter Thirteen

Moral leadership style

In recent times we have seen some shocking scandals involving leaders in church and state. People feel a great sense of betrayal that those they trusted have behaved in such a despicable manner. More than ever we need a return to moral values in leadership. This final chapter briefly explores some of the important points for such leadership.

A leader, by definition, is one who guides, who shows the way by example. (Webster)[1] A leader must have the ability to persuade others. If there is no persuasion, there simply is no leadership. In order to be able to persuade others to follow a course of action; a leader must have personal integrity.

If a leader cannot be trusted, he/she cannot lead, for the populous will not be guided by someone in whom they have no confidence.

1 www.forbes.com/.../20-leadership-quotes-to-make-you-laugh

Moral leadership is a different kind of leadership. Moral leaders aim to serve.

They tend to develop the capacities of others.

Moral leadership is not about rank – any person holding any position can be a moral leader, but such individuals are always characterised by a deep sense of ethics, are driven by core ideals (such as justice) and are motivated by the pursuit of a higher purpose.[2]

Moral leaders are people of character who function by natural principles; and build these principles into their lives, their relationships, their management processes and mission statements.

Moral leadership involves leading in a manner that respects the rights and dignity of others. As leaders are in a position of social power, moral leadership focuses on how leaders use their social power in the decisions they make, actions they engage in and ways they influence others. [3]

They use their social power to serve the greater good instead of self-serving interests.

Moral leadership is also about particular capacities and skills.

First of all, moral leaders know how to manage themselves, how to act with nobility and rectitude.

They are visionary and affect personal change.[4]

Moral leaders also have a highly developed sense of emotional intelligence and master key social skills.

They work to overcome obstacles and are skilled at the art of consultation.[5] They build consensus see for diversity and establish unity.

2   Stephen www.globalethicsnetwork.org/.../what-do-you-mean-by-moral-leadership
3   Stephen www.globalethicsnetwork.org/.../what-do-you-mean-by-moral-leadership
4   Stephen www.globalethicsnetwork.org/.../what-do-you-mean-by-moral-leadership
5   Stephen www.globalethicsnetwork.org/.../what-do-you-mean-by-moral-leadership

Moral leaders are the conscience (i.e. moral compass) of an enterprise or organisation and the glue that holds it together.[6]

Leadership in public gaze[7]

Morality in leadership matters a lot. The moment you accept a leadership position, you have to be prepared to be in public gaze. Your conduct needs to be impeccable. What you say and do needs to be measured.

As a leader, you are accountable to society at large. Leadership, therefore, comes with responsibilities. [8]

Moral leadership is about looking at yourself in the mirror and being able to tell yourself that you have done the right thing.[9] It is about being able to live with your choices, when these are tested against values and not against regulation and results.

Principle–centred Leadership

Stephen Covey describes the importance of principle-centred leadership thus: 'correct principles are like compasses: they are always pointing the way. And if we know how to read them, we won't get lost, confused or fooled by conflicting voices and values.[10] Principles are self- evident, self –validating natural laws. They don't change or shift. They provide 'true north' direction to our lives when navigating the streams of our environments. Principles apply at all times in all places.

They surface in the form of values, ideas, norms and teachings that uplift, ennoble, fulfil, empower and inspire people.

6   Stephen www.globalethicsnetwork.org/.../what-do-you-mean-by-moral-leadership
7   What do you mean by Moral Leadership? - Global Ethics Network www.globalethicsnetwork.
    org/xn/detail/6428686:BlogPost:26062?xg8
8   www.globalethicsnetwork.org/xn/detail/6428686:BlogPost:26062?xg8
9   www.globalethicsnetwork.org/xn/detail/6428686:BlogPost:26062?xg8
10 Stephen Covey, 1990 Principle centred leadership, p19.

The lesson of history is that to the degree people and civilizations have operated in harmony with correct principles, they have prospered. At the root of societal declines are foolish practices that represent violations of correct principles.'[11]

Moral leadership helps followers to see the real conflict between competing values, between espoused values and behaviour. In describing transformational leadership, Covey used words such as developer, mentor, value, clarifier and exemplar. [12]

These leaders cultivate collaborative relationships based on mutual interests what we call win-win. Because Covey believes transformational leadership builds on the need for meaning, he also uses words like purpose, values, love, moral, ethics, mission and principles to clarify this type of leadership.

He says that becoming a transformational leader requires vision, initiative, patience, respect, courage and faith.[13]

Leading by morals[14]

Leading by morals requires a different mindset. It is practiced from inside out on four levels. [15]

1. Personal: one's relationship with oneself.

2. Interpersonal: one's relationship and interaction with others.

3. Managerial: one's responsibility to get a job done with others.

4. Organisational: one's need to organise people, to recruit, train, build teams, create aligned structure, strategy and system.

11 ibid p.19
12 ibid p.19
13 ibid p.19
14 P.T. Joseph, 2010 Pastoral Leadership styles p.278.
15 ibid p.279.

Moral leadership is based on the reality that we cannot violate these natural laws with impunity. There are no quick fixes to inter-personal issues. Individuals and organisations are more empowered when governed by proven principles.

Moral principles are objective and external. They operate in obedience to natural laws, regardless of conditions. [16]

Moral leaders set a moral tone that is not only pervasive but also possible. Principle–centred leaders tend to have clear boundaries. They show this by clearly setting up tasks, responsibilities and reporting relationships.

This leads to strong, directive control over those who work for them. Delegating is seen as risky since it opens up the possibility that the work won't be up to the mark. There is always a sense they could do better than anyone else. They like schedules and lists are orderly and have a great eye for details.

Most of us idolize leaders like Mahatma Gandhi, Nelson Mandela and lament about the lack of leadership and role models today. We need to look around ourselves and we will find modern day heroes in those leaders who believe in moral leadership. We can be the moral leaders and the heroes for a new generation. The choice is ours.

Chapter Fourteen

Conclusions

"LIfe is like a dogsled team. If you ain't the lead dog, the scenery never changes." - Lewis Grizzard[1]

Vision is everything for a leader. Vision leads the leader and paints the target for moving forward. A leader without vision is just travelling in a circle. Leadership vision comes from within oneself and draws on our natural gifts and desires.

Our personal vision draws on our history.

It grows from our past and the people around us. True vision will meet the needs of others and will go beyond what one individual can achieve. It is not just about including others, it is about adding value to them and helping them blossom.

Every training workshop I give on leadership I ask the participants to name leaders they admire.

1   www.brainyquote.com/quotes/authors/r/robert_martin.

Then I ask them to examine why they admire these particular leaders and tell the group what qualities they see in them.

Having listed these qualities I ask each participant to focus on how many of these qualities are in them. We recognize qualities in others because they are in ourselves. Vision is like a magnet attracting people to follow us. It challenges, unites, attracts finances and resources.

The greater the vision, the more winners it has the potential to attract. It is an interesting fact that the more challenging the vision is, the harder the participants fight to achieve it. As you read this ask yourself; what stirs your own heart? What do you dream about? What would you like to change in the world?

Positive people

Gather people around you who are positive, listen to different voices and opinions as you develop your own vision. Nobody can accomplish great things alone, we need a good team.

We all need good advice from someone who is ahead of us in the leadership journey. If you want to lead others to greatness find a mentor.

Measure yourself. Talk to others about what you are doing and the vision you have for life. If they can articulate it then you are probably living it.

No leader goes on forever and those who try to do so become dictators and sometimes turn into despots, destroying the good they might have done earlier on in their leadership journey.

The greatest misunderstanding about leadership is that is based on position. It is not the position that makes the leader but the leader that makes the position. You can lose your position but still maintain your leadership.

Our leadership success is not measured by what we are leaving to but by what we are leaving behind. We will be judged by how well people do after we leave. Our lasting value is measured by succession. In my own life, I have found having a sense of humour central to leadership.

Taking oneself too seriously is never good for the health. I've put a lot of work into building relationships and networks. In doing this I am reminded of a quote by Robert Martin 'taking an interest in what others are thinking and doing is often a much more powerful form of encouragement and praise.'[2]

In leading I know my life's work fits into a broader, more significant context than just me. Graveyards are full of people who believed they couldn't be done without. I need a sense of meaning in life. I live and lead with my own strengths.

I realise I cannot be all things to all people if I am to remain effective. I work with what I have control over and when I cannot change a situation I change my attitude and approach towards it. I make my own luck by not letting failures define me.

Jim Loehr, co-author of the Harvard Business Review article entitled 'The Making of a Corporate Athlete,'[3] describes an ideal performance state as prolonged and sustained high performance over time.

To do this one has to take care of one's own life to keep burnout at bay. Years ago a friend said to me 'Make an appointment with yourself everyday and put it in your diary.'

Over to you

There is an old story about three frogs sitting on a log and one of them decides to jump.[4]

2 hbr.org/2001/01/the-making-of-a-corporate-athlete /ar/1
3 www.cpco.on.ca/CatholicCommunity/prayers/leaderprayer
4 http://websitesgiveback.com/blog/three-frogs-sitting-on-a-log

The question is asked, "How many are left?" The answer is "three". He only decided to jump, he didn't jump and that is the point.

In the sport of tennis a good follow through is important in delivering the ball to the opponent's side of the court. In using tennis as a metaphor to talk about leadership it helps to remember that a powerful serve is not always the most effective strategy to defeat our opponent, sometime a good cross court shot is just as effective in winning a point and the game.

As leaders we can think strategically about doing something but until we follow through with action nothing happens. It's now up to you to take up leadership where you are. Let me finish with a paraphrase of a leaders' prayer.

Leadership is hard to define. Let us be the ones who define it with justice. Leadership is like a handful of water. Let us be the people to share it with those who thirst. Leadership is not about watching and correcting. Let us remember it is about listening and connecting.

Leadership is not about telling people what to do. Let us find out what people want. Leadership is less about the love of power and more about the power of love. As we continue to undertake the role of leader let us be affirmed by the servant leadership. Let our greatest passion be compassion and our greatest strength be love.

Let our greatest victory be the reward of peace. In leading let us never fail to follow. In loving let us never fail those we lead.[5]

You are today where your thoughts have brought you; you will be tomorrow where your thoughts take you[6].

5 www.cpco.on.ca/CatholicCommunity/prayers/leaderprayer. pdf
6 James Allen, 1864-1912 www.brainyquote.com/quotes/quotes/j/jamesallen133802

Bibliography

1. Beney, P. (2005, edition) The Majesty of Charlesto, p.64. Saxton, Eugene. "St. Giovanni Melchior Bosco." The Catholic Encyclopaedia, Vol. 2.Bosco, Third Edition. New Rochelle: Don Bosco Publications

2. Bass, B. M. (1985). Leadership and performance beyond expectation. New York: Free Press.

3. Bass, B. M. (1990). 'From transactional to transformational leadership: Learning to share the Vision.' Organizational Dynamics, (winter): 19-31.

4. Burns, J. M. (1978) Leadership. New York: Harper & Row

5. Bartlett, F. C (1926) 'The social Psychology of leadership', Journal of the National Institute of Industrial Psychology 3:188-193

6. Bolman, L. G. & Deal, T. E. (2003). Reframing organizations. San   Francisco: Josey-Bass Publishers.

7. Blanchard, Ken, John P. Carlos, Alan Randolph, keys to Empowerment , Berrett-Koehler, 12 Apr 1999 - Business & Economics .

8. Brandau, Karla, The Charismatic Leader – Diamond Performance. Workplace Power Institutewww.leadingtoday.org/Onmag/2012%20Archives/.../kb-january12.pdf

9. 'Charismatic domination' Wikipedia, Jan 24, 2014 http://. Wikipedia.org/wiki/charismatic domination

10. Collins, J. (2001). Good to Great, London: Random House

11. Fiedler, Fred (1967) A Theory of Leadership Effectiveness US: University of Washington

12. Lao Tzu, Tao Te Ching, (Translated by Gia-Fu Feng and Jane English) Aldershot UK

13. Conference Reference: The Preventive system international conference on Human rights, Rome, 2nd to 6th January 2009.

14. Covey Stephen, (1990) Principled Centred Leadership, New York: Simon and Schuster

15. Finnegan, J. (October 2012), Don Bosco Educator: p.6 and p.8, Lecture given as part of Bi-Centenary (www.donbosco.org

16. Greenleaf, Robert K. Servant Leadership: A Journey into the Nature of Legitimate Power and Greatness. In-

dianapolis: The Robert K. Greenleaf Center, 1970.

17. Handy, C. (1999), Understanding Organisations,

18. 4th Edition. London: Penguin Publications.

19. Heifetz , Ronald A, Linsky Marty,(2002), Leadership on the line, Staying alive through the dangers of leading. Boston Massachusetts: Harvard Business Press

20. Haslam, Alexander, S, Reicher Stephen D, Platlow, Michael J, (2011), The New Psychology of Leadership, Identity, Influence and Power, Hove and New York: Psychology Press, Taylor & Francis Group.

21. Hodges, Phil, (2007)   Like Jesus: Lessons from the Greatest Leadership Role Model of All Time, Thomas Nelson.

22. Kouzes, J & Posner, B, (2010), San Francisco: Jossey –Bass

23. Joseph, P.T. (2010), Pastoral Leadership Styles and Emotional Intelligence, Bombay: St Paul's Society,

24. Lawrence, T E (1888-1935) Seven Pillars of Wisdom

25. A Project Gutenberg: Wordsworth Editions, 1997

26. Lemoyne, G.B. (1966). The Biographical Memoirs of Saint John Bosco, Vol. 2, 1841-1846 New Rochelle: Salesian Publishers, Inc.

27. Lemoyne, G.B. (1966) The Biographical Memoirs of Saint John Bosco, Vol. 3 1847-1849 New Rochelle: Salesian Publishers Inc.

28. Lenti, J. A. (2007), Vol 2. Don Bosco History and Spir-

it -Birth and early development of Don Bosco's Oratory. Rome: Liberia Ateneo Salesiano,

29. Lenti, J. A. (2008), Vol 3. Don Bosco History and Spirit, Don Bosco educator, spiritual master, writer and founder of the Salesian Society, Rome: Liberia Ateneo Salesiano,

30. Lenti J. A. (2008), Vol 4. Don Bosco History and Spirit, Beginnings of the Salesian Society and its Constitution. Rome: Liberia Ateneo Salesiano

31. Mandela, Nelson (1995), Long Walk to Freedom. Back Bay Books 237 Park Avenue, New York

32. Meyer, J. and Rowan, B. (1983). "Institutionalized Organizations: Formal Structure as Myth and Ceremony" in J. Meyer and W. Scott (eds.), Organizational Environments: Ritual and Rationality. CA Thousand Oaks: Sage.

33. Memoirs of the Oratory of St.Francis de Sales from 1815-1855: The Autobiography of Saint John Bosco (1989) Translated by D. Lyons. New Rochelle: Don Bosco Publications

34. McMillen, S.I., David E., M.D. Stern None of These Diseases Paperback – (June 1, 1984), Fleming H Revell Cambridge University Press

35. Mitchell, T R. (1971/74) A Path-Goal Theory of Leader Effectiveness, Robert House, University of Pennsylvania

36. Morrison, John, A, (1979), The Educational philosophy of St. John Bosco, New Rochelle, New York: Liberia Ateneo Salesiano,

37. Palmer, J Parker, (2000), Let your life speak, listening to the voice of vocation. Jossey –Bass, San Francisco.

38. Ramzey S. Chehab. May 10, (2006) - The Art of Leadership (Google eBook) Author House.

39. Ruth, Sean, (2006), Leadership and Liberation, A psychological approach, Hove, East Sussex: Routledge

40. Spears, L, 2002, March 'Tracing the past, present and future of Servant-leadership' in L Spears & M Lawrence, Focus on leadership: Servant –Leadership for the 21st Century, New York: John Wiley & Sons

41. Stella, Pietro, (1985), Don Bosco Life and work, Translated by John Drury, New Rochelle, New York: Don Bosco Publications

42. Tannenbaum, A.S. and Schmitt, W.H. (1958) How to choose a Leadership pattern, Maier, N.R.F. (1963). Problem-solving discussions and conferences: Leadership methods and skills. New York: McGraw-Hill

43. Tannenbaum, Robert and Warren Schmidt, (1958) How to Choose a Leadership Pattern, US: Harvard Business Review article.

44. Weber M. (1946) The sociology of charismatic authority. In H.H. Gerth & C.W. Milles (Trans & Eds) Max Weber: Essays in sociology (pp.245-252) New York: Oxford University Press (Original work published 1922)

45. Yukl, G. A. (1989). Leadership in Organizations. Englewood Cliffs, NJ: Prentice Hall.

46. Web pages:

47. www.sdb.org › Salesian Family.

48. Website: http://www.jonathanfarrington.com

49. http// cbae.nmsu. edu/-dboje/teaching/338 transformational leadership htm

50. http://www.goodreads.com/quotes/tag/leadership

51. http://www.brightquotes.com/lea_fr.html

52. http://management.about.com/cs/generalmanagement/a/Pareto081202.htm

53. http://www.evancarmichael.com/Management/5182/Leadership-Styles--3-Key-Lessons-From-the-Hard-Man-Who-Found-His-Heart.

54. http://www.christianpost.com/news/the-principle-of-the-leadership-lid-45905/

55. http://www.learn-to-be-a-leader.com/leadership-theories.html

56. lifelessons4u.wordpress.com/tag/al-pacinos-inspirational-speech/

57. .http://www.leadingtoday.org/Onmag/2012%20Archives/Jan%2012/kb-january12.pdf

58. Institutewww.leadingtoday.org/Onmag/2012%20Archives/.../kb-january12.pdf

Notes

www.ingramcontent.com/pod-product-compliance
Lightning Source LLC
Chambersburg PA
CBHW051725040426
42447CB00008B/987